Collins *gem*

Clans &
Tartans

HarperCollins*Publishers*
Westerhill Road, Bishopbriggs, Glasgow G64 2QT

www.collins.co.uk

First published 1986
This edition published 2005

Reprint 10 9 8 7 6 5 4

© HarperCollins Publishers 1986, 2005

ISBN 13: 978 0 00 717855-1

The tartans illustrated in this book were reproduced directly
from cloth supplied by Peter MacArthur & Co. Ltd of
Hamilton, to whom the publishers are greatly indebted.
Printed in China

Contents

The History of Tartan

The antiquity of tartan is amply proved by the many references to it in early Scottish literature and in the written accounts of travellers who visited Scotland several hundreds of years ago. The ancient method of describing it was to refer to it as 'mottled', 'striped', 'sundrie coloured', 'marled', and so on, but the Gaelic word for tartan is *breacan*, meaning chequered, and is aptly descriptive of the check-like arrangement of tartan patterns. When we refer to the 'sett' of a tartan, we mean the pattern, and a length of tartan is made up of one sett repeated over and over again until the desired length is made.

For many centuries tartan formed part of the everyday garb of the Highland people, and while it was also worn in other parts of Scotland it was in the Highlands that its use continued and developed until it became recognised as a symbol of clan kinship. The articles of dress for which tartan was used, such as the belted plaids, the *philabeg*, or kilt, and the trews, are well known. With these were worn shoes of untanned hide and the *cuaran*, a boot which reached almost to the knee, made of horse or cow hide shaped to the leg and kept in position with thongs. It was also a common practice to go bare-legged and bare-footed. A bonnet of knitted wool was generally worn, with a badge common to the clan, generally a flower or plant. The sporran worn in front of the kilt to serve as a purse was usually made of leather and often highly ornamented.

The women wore a *curraichd* of linen over their heads, fastened under the chin. The *tonnag* was a small square of tartan worn over the shoulders, and the *arasaid* was a long garment of various colours or of tartan, reaching from the head or neck to the ankles, pleated all round, fastened at the breast with a large brooch and at the waist by a belt.

It is believed that the tartans used several centuries ago were simple checks of two or three colours and that these

5

colours were obtained from the dye-producing plants, roots, berries and trees found in the districts where the cloth was woven. These simple checks were district tartans and were worn by the people of the district where they were made. As the people inhabiting a district were generally members of the same clan, their district tartan was, in effect, a clan tartan. Martin Martin in his *Description of the Western Islands of Scotland*, completed circa 1695 and published in 1703, tells us, 'Every Isle differs from each other in their fancy of making Plads, as to the Stripes in Breadth and Colours. This Humour is as different thro the main Land of the Highlands, in-so-far that they who have seen those Places, are able, at the first view of a Man's Plad, to guess the Place of his Residence....'

The same writer also tells us that weavers took great pains to give exact patterns of the tartan by having the number and colour of every thread upon a piece of wood known as a *maide dalbh*, or pattern stick, which served as a guide for the weaver.

When chemical dyes came into use weavers were able to enlarge their range of colours and more elaborate patterns were introduced. It is believed that as time passed branches of the larger clans evolved tartans of their own by adding an overstripe or other variation to the basic pattern of their parent clan.

What may be one of the earliest references to the royal use of tartan is contained in the accounts of the treasurer to King James III in 1471, where mention is made of tartan purchased for the King and Queen. King James V wore tartan when hunting in the Highlands in 1538, and King Charles II wore tartan ribbons on his coat at his marriage in 1662.

In a Crown charter of 1587, to Hector MacLean of Duart, the feu duty payable on the lands of Narraboll, Islay, was sixty ells of cloth of white, black and green colours. These colours correspond to the colours in the tartan we now call MacLean Hunting, but it is doubtful if their arrangement was exactly the same as that in use now. This may be the first clan tartan.

The antiquity of tartan has never been doubted, but some critics aver that the wearing of a particular pattern by all the members of a clan as a common clan tartan is a modern custom dating no earlier than the late 18th century. They also claim that prior to that period there were no definite tartans and that clansmen wore whatever patterns the weavers chose to supply.

From the archives of a Highland burgh, we learn that southern merchants came to the Highlands to purchase tartan in the 16th and 17th centuries, and the baillies of that burgh, to prevent overcharging, fixed maximum prices for tartan, the prices being determined by the number and shades of colours in the cloth. In the same records we read of a housewife who, in 1572, gave coloured wool to a weaver to make into cloth. In suing him before the magistrates, she accused him of making the pattern according to his 'awin fasoun' (own fashion) and not according to her instructions. She won her case, and the weaver was punished. By her action she has proved that Highland housewives were not prepared to accept, without question, whatever patterns weavers provided.

In other literary sources we read of clansmen dressed in the livery of their chiefs, and it is reasonable to infer that the livery was tartan. One of the best-known instances is the accusation of Lady Grange, who claimed that her abductors, in 1732, were dressed in Lord Lovat's livery. It is known that the clans were organized on military lines, and that there were clan regiments. In 1704 the fencible men of Clan Grant in Strathspey were ordered to rendezvous and to have 'ilk ane of thame Heighland coates, trewes, and shorthose of tartan of red and greine sett broad-springed....' This company of men were all dressed in the same tartan, and there is reason to believe that other clan regiments were dressed in the tartan or 'livery' of their chief.

After the Battle of Culloden in 1746, the government in London, in an endeavour to purge the Highlands of all unlawful elements, passed an Act of Parliament whereby the Highlander was disarmed and the wearing of tartan made a penal offence. This Act was rigorously enforced and the anxiety of the government to abolish tartan and the Highland dress suggests that they held more than sentimental meaning for the Highland people.

By the time the Act was repealed in 1785, Highlanders had become accustomed to wearing the same type of dress as other Scots, and they showed no great enthusiasm, even if they could afford to do so, to don tartan clothing. Tartan was almost a thing of the past; many of the old weavers had died, and with their passing details of old patterns were lost; the wooden pattern sticks had rotted away, and such fragments of old tartan cloth as remained were so worn and perished they were of little value in adding to the little knowledge that remained of pre-1745 tartans.

The first great tartan revival took place in 1822. George IV, when visiting Edinburgh in that year, suggested that the people should attend the functions wearing their respective tartans. Unfortunately, this resulted in many 'original' tartans being made, since those who had no tartan could always find a tailor to invent one for them. The publication of a book, *Vestiarium Scoticum*, by the brothers Sobieski Stuart helped to augment the number of spurious tartans, and indeed many tartans existing today owe their existence to this book, although much doubt has been cast on its authenticity. Other 19th-century publications added to the confusion but, unlike the *Vestiarium*, they made no claim to antiquity regarding the tartans they exhibited.

Today the confusion of past uncertainty is being regulated into some semblance of order, and patterns are being standardized into recognized settings. The registration of tartans in the Registers at Lyon Court should do much to avoid confusion in the future.

Tartans are described according to the purpose for which they are named.

Clan tartans are patterns for general use by clanspeople. It is not uncommon to find a clan tartan of recent origin described as 'ancient clan tartan'. The use of the word 'ancient' is most misleading as it is merely an indication that the tartan has been woven in lighter-coloured shades.

Dress tartans were originally worn by the women of the clan who preferred lighter-coloured patterns. They had a white background and were variations of the clan pattern. In recent years there has been a tendency to refer to clan tartans woven in lightweight materials as 'dress' tartan. This causes confusion and should be avoided. Clans who do not possess a dress tartan usually wear the clan pattern, in lightweight material, for evening wear, but this does not justify the description of a clan tartan as a 'dress' tartan.

Mourning tartans at one time were worn for the purpose for which they were named. They were generally of black and white.

Hunting tartans are worn for sport and outdoor activities. Brown or some other dark hue is the predominant colour. When a clan possessed a brightly coloured tartan it was unsuitable for hunting purposes, and hunting setts were devised to make the wearer less conspicuous. The colours were arranged so that, when concealed in the heather, the tartan blended with the surroundings.

Chiefs' tartans are the personal tartans of the chiefs and should never be worn except by the chief and his immediate family.

While tartan continues to excite the admiration of people everywhere, it is impossible to lay down hard and fast rules regarding choice of tartans. In all probability the would-be wearer of tartan will select the 'tartan of his fancy'. One caution may be voiced. The royal tartans are for the use of the royal family and should not be worn by anyone outside the royal family.

This map gives approximate location of the Clans and Families of Scotland. Territories located outside the Highland Line (that invisible boundary forming the division between the Highlands and the rest of Scotland) have been determined by reference to reliable records and manuscripts. On a small scale map it is possible to indicate only the most prominent names. Absence of any family does not mean that they are landless.

N
E
W
S

SINCLAIR
Thurso
GUNN
KEITH
MURRAY
MACKAY
SUTHERLAND
ROSS
MUNRO
BRODIE
INNES KEITH
HAY
MACLEOD
MACNICOL
URQUHART
ROSE
Inverness
GORDON
LESLIE
SKENE
Aberdeen
MACKENZIE
FRASER
MACLEAN
MACINTOSH
DAVIDSON
FORBES
BARCLAY
MACDONELL
OF GLENGARRY
MACLEOD
OF LEWIS
GRANT
MATHESON
CHISHOLM
MACGILLIVRAY
COMYN
SHAW
Balmoral
FARQUHARSON
LINDSAY
OGILVIE
MORRISON
MACLEOD
OF LEWIS
MACKENZIE
MACAULEY
MACIVER
MACLEOD
OF HARRIS
MACQUEEN
Isle of Skye
MACLEOD
OF SKYE
MACKINNON
MACINNES
MACRAE
MACLENNAN
NOSBERRIE
CUMMING
ROBERTSON
STEWART
GOW
MURRAY
MENZIES
Fort
William
CAMERON
MACDONELL
KEPPOCH
MACDONALD
OF GLENGARRY
MACDONALD
OF HARRIS
N. Uist
MACDONALD
MACDONALD
OF
CLANRANALD
S. Uist
CLANRANALD
Canna
Rum
Egg
Muck
MACDONALD
CLANRANALD
MACLEAN
MACNEILL
Barra
Coll

Anderson or MacAndrew

Crest Badge: *An oak tree proper.*

Motto: *Stand sure.*

Gaelic Name: *Mac Ghille Aindrais.*

This name, now fairly widespread in Scotland, means 'son of Andrew'. In the Highlands it is usually found as MacAndrew while in the Lowlands the Anderson form is more common. Some MacAndrews are traditionally associated with the MacDonells of Glengarry and wear their tartan, but the clan is generally regarded as a sept of Clan Chattan, having been associated with that confederation from the beginning of the 15th century. In the Kinrara Manuscript it is claimed that the MacAndrews came east to Badenoch from Moidart about 1400. A famous member of the clan was John MacAndrew of Dalnahatnich, known in Gaelic as Iain Beg MacAindrea. He was a noted bowman, and many tales are told of his exploits. In 1670 some Lochaber men raided Badenoch and drove away a large number of cattle. They were pursued and overtaken by a body of men including Iain Beg, and in the fight which followed Iain Beg killed most of the raiders. Only one Lochaber man escaped to carry with him the story of his comrades' fate at the hands of Iain Beg MacAindrea. The men of Lochaber swore vengeance against 'little John' and made many attempts on his life. As a result, for many years he had to live an unsettled existence but was always able to defend himself.

The most prominent branches of the Andersons were Dowhill, Wester Ardbreck and Candacraig in Strathdon, Aberdeenshire.

Armstrong

Crest Badge: *An arm embowed, proper.*

Motto: *Invictus maneo (I remain unvanquished).*

Gaelic Name: *Mac Ghillielàidir.*

According to an act passed by the Scottish Parliament in 1587, as long ago as the 16th century Border families were described as clans. 'For the quieting and keeping in obedience of the ... inhabitants of the Borders, Highlands and Isles', runs the act, which contains a roll of 'the clans that have Captains, Chiefs and Chieftains ... as well on the Borders as the Highlands'. One of the most important and notorious of these Border families was the Armstrongs.

The story goes that the progenitor of the clan was one Fairbairn, armour bearer to a Scottish king, who went to the king's assistance when his horse was killed under him in battle. For this service the king granted Fairbairn lands on the Borders, and named him Armstrong.

The first family of the name on record is found in Liddesdale in 1376, and while the Armstrongs held lands all along the Borders, here their power was unquestionable. They could muster 3,000 men at a time, and their lawlessness kept the Borders in turmoil.

The Armstrongs of Gilnockie were the principal branch of the clan, and in the early part of the 16th century John Armstrong of Gilnockie and over thirty of his followers were hanged by James V at Carlingrigg. This event is the subject of one of the best-known Border ballads.

Baird

Crest Badge: *An eagle's head erased, proper.*

Motto: *Dominus fecit*
(The Lord made).

Gaelic Name: *Mac a'bhaird.*

The name Baird comes from the Gaelic word for a poet. The fortunes of the clan were started in the reign of William I, 'The Lion', when he made extensive grants to a member of the clan who had saved his life from a wild boar. Later, a charter was granted to Richard Baird of Meikle and Little Kyp in Lanarkshire, and in the early 14th century Robert the Bruce granted the Barony of Cambusnethan, also in Lanarkshire, to a Robert Baird. This family of Cambusnethan spread north to Banffshire, and later east to Auchmeddan in Aberdeenshire. George Baird of Auchmeddan married the niece of the Earl Marischal and the family increased in importance in Aberdeenshire, supplying many sheriffs. From the Auchmeddan branch come the Bairds of Newbyth and Saughtonhall in East Lothian.

The Bairds produced some notable leaders. General Sir David Baird from Newbyth served in India where he was one of only two survivors of the 73rd Highland Regiment at the defeat of British forces in 1780. After four years' imprisonment, he went on to command at the capture of Seringapatam in 1799. He captured the Cape of Good Hope from the Dutch in 1806, and was at the siege of Copenhagen in 1807. He was Sir John Moore's second-in-command at Corunna in 1808, and after Moore's death assumed command. James and William Baird of Gartsherrie established the largest of Scotland's iron companies in the 1830s, producing a quarter of the country's iron.

Barclay

Crest Badge: *Out of a chapeau azure turned ermine a hand holding a dagger, proper.*

Motto: *Aut agere aut mori (Either action or death).*

The Barclays in Scotland are claimed to be descended from the Berkeleys who came to England with William the Conqueror. In 1165 Walter de Berkeley was Chamberlain of Scotland, and in the 12th and 13th centuries the Berkeleys were numerous in Kincardineshire and the East of Scotland. The Barclays of Mathers in Kincardineshire traced their descent from Alexander, who obtained these lands in 1351 on his marriage to the sister of the Earl Marischal of Scotland. His son was the first of the clan to spell his name in the modern way. The lands remained in the possession of the family until David Barclay, born in 1580, was compelled to sell his estates. The chiefship passed to the descendants of James Barclay of Mill of Towie in the 19th century.

The Barclays of Urie are descended from Colonel David Barclay, who had served under Gustavus Adolphus of Sweden, and who purchased the estate of Urie in 1647. Robert, his eldest son, became a celebrated Quaker. In 1682 he was appointed governor of New Jersey, but did not take up residence, although his brother John settled there.

Other important branches of the family were the Barclays of Collairnie in Fife, of Pierston, and of Ardrossan. The Barclays of Tolly, in Aberdeenshire, retained possession of their lands from the 12th until the 18th century, and from this family was descended the famous Russian General, Field Marshall Prince Barclay de Tolly, who died in 1818.

Brodie

Crest Badge: *A dexter hand holding a sheaf of arrows, all proper.*

Motto: *Unite.*

Gaelic Name: *Brothaigh.*

From earliest times the Clan Brodie was associated with the ancient province of Moray. In the 12th century Malcolm IV is said to have confirmed their possession of land there, and Michael, Thane of Brodie, received a charter from Robert the Bruce two or three years before the battle of Bannockburn. During the 13th, 14th and 15th centuries the family name appears frequently in charters of the period, and John of Brodie assisted the MacKenzies against the MacDonalds at the battle of Blair-na-park in 1466. In 1550 Alexander Brodie and over a hundred others were denounced as rebels for attacking Alexander Cumming of Altyre.

The family continued prominent in local and national affairs and Alexander Brodie of Brodie, born in 1617, was a senator of the College of Justice. He represented the county of Elgin in Parliament from 1643, and in 1649 he went to Holland to treat with Charles II and to arrange for the conditions of his return to Scotland. He was called to London by Cromwell to negotiate a union between the two kingdoms, but he avoided employment under the Lord-Protector. He died in 1679. Alexander Brodie of Brodie, born in 1697, was appointed Lord Lyon King at Arms in 1727. Throughout the long history of the family the Brodies became connected through marriage with many of the greatest families in Scotland. The seat of the chief is Brodie Castle in Morayshire.

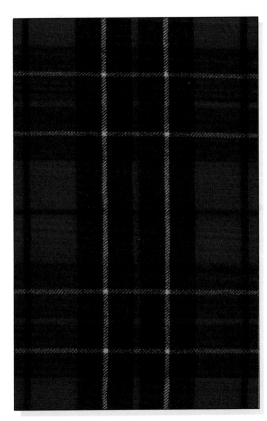

Bruce

Crest Badge: *A lion statant with tail extended, azure, armed and langued gules.*

Motto: *Fuimus* (We have been).

Gaelic Name: *Brus.*

Sir Robert de Brus, a Norman knight who accompanied William the Conqueror to England in 1066, is claimed as the progenitor of this clan. The connection of the Brus family with Scotland originated when Robert de Brus was companion at arms to Prince David, later David I, during his stay at the court of Henry I of England. Brus received from David a grant of the Lordship of Annandale. He resigned his lands to his son at the outbreak of war with England, and at the Battle of the Standard in 1138, the elder Brus, who fought on the English side, is said to have taken his own son prisoner. Robert, 4th Lord of Annandale, married a niece of William I, The Lion, and it was on this marriage that the subsequent claims of the family of Bruce to the throne of Scotland were based. Robert, 6th Lord of Annandale and 1st Earl of Carrick, maintained his claims, but fought on the English side at the Battle of Dunbar in 1296. He died in 1304.

His eldest son Robert, 7th Lord of Annandale and 2nd Earl of Carrick, was born in 1274. He was the famous Robert the Bruce, victor of Bannockburn in 1314, who, after a fierce struggle, gained Scotland's independence from England, acknowledged by the Treaty of Northampton in 1328. He died in 1329 at Cardross in Dunbartonshire. His body was buried in Dunfermline and his heart in Melrose.

The Earls of Elgin are descended from the Bruces of Clackmannan.

Buchanan

Crest Badge: *A dexter hand couped at the wrist, holding up a chapeau tasseled with a rose gules, all within a laurel wreath, proper.*

Motto: *Clarior hinc honos (Brighter hence the honour).*

Gaelic Name: *Canonach.*

Buchanan of Auchmar traces the origin of the clan to Anselan o'Kyan, son of a king of Ulster, who landed in Argyll in about 1016. For his services against the Danes, so it is said, he received from Malcolm II the lands of Buchanan, to the east of Loch Lomond. These lands remained in the possession of the family for almost seven centuries until the death of John, 22nd laird of Buchanan, in 1682. Cadets of the clan included the Buchanans of Auchmar, Spittal, Arnprior, Drumikill, Carbeth and Leny, and the chiefship passed to the Leny branch.

The clan supported Robert the Bruce in his struggle for Scottish independence and was represented among the 7,000 men sent from Scotland to assist the French king after the Battle of Agincourt. It is claimed that Sir Alexander Buchanan killed the Duke of Clarence at the Battle of Bauge in 1421.

The chief of the clan and Buchanan of Leny fell at Flodden in 1513, and the clan took an active part in the Battle of Pinkie in 1547 and at Langside in 1568. The Buchanan lands were sold in 1682 and the principal line became extinct in 1762. The chiefship then passed to Buchanan of Spittal.

George Buchanan, the famous Latin scholar, was tutor to both Mary Queen of Scots and James VI and from 1570 until 1578 Keeper of the Privy Seal.

Cameron

Crest Badge: *A sheaf of five arrows tied with a band, gules.*

Motto: *Aonaibh ri cheile (Unite).*

Gaelic Name: Camshron.

The Clan Cameron, described as 'fiercer than fierceness itself', is reputed to be one of the ancient clans of Scotland. It consisted originally of three branches, the MacMartins of Letterfinlay, the MacGillonies of Strone, and the MacSorlies of Glen Nevis. The Camerons of Lochiel descended from the Strone branch and are said to have obtained their lands and the chiefship of the clan through intermarriage with the Letterfinlay branch. For a time the clan were subject to the Lords of the Isles and assisted Donald, Lord of the Isles, at the Battle of Harlaw in 1411. Later, however, the Camerons withdrew from their association with their powerful allies and a long period of feuds followed.

A notable chief was Sir Ewen of Lochiel, born in 1629, who was received in London by Charles II in 1660, and was knighted in 1680. Ten years later, he fought at Killiecrankie. In 1715, when too old for military service, Sir Ewen sent the clan, under his son, to help the Earl of Mar in the Jacobite cause. Sir Ewen's grandson Donald, known as 'the Gentle Lochiel', joined Prince Charles in 1745, and was one of the outstanding personalities of that Rising. Although wounded at Culloden, he managed to escape to France and died there in 1748. The family estates were forfeited, but on their restoration under the General Act of Amnesty of 1748, the Gentle Lochiel's grandson, Donald, 22nd chief, resumed possession.

Campbell

Crest Badge: *A boar's head, fesswise, couped, or.*

Motto: *Ne obliviscaris (Forget not).*

Gaelic Name: *Caimbeul.*

Known as the 'race of Diarmid', the Clan Campbell was for centuries a most powerful influence in Argyll and the West of Scotland. In the 13th century Archibald Campbell obtained the Lordship of Lochow through his marriage with the daughter of the King's Treasurer, and for a long period thereafter the Campbells of Lochow formed one of the chief branches of the clan.

Sir Colin of Lochow, progenitor of the Campbells of Argyll, was knighted in 1280, and from him the chiefs of Argyll received the designation MacCailean Mor. A descendant, Sir Duncan, was created a peer by James II in 1445 and Duncan's grandson Colin made Earl of Argyll in 1457. Archibald, his son, who was Lord High Chancellor, was killed at Flodden in 1513.

Archibald, 5th Earl, although a prominent Reformer, commanded the army of Queen Mary at the Battle of Langside in 1568, while his brother Colin supported the young King James. Archibald, 7th Earl, commanded the army which was defeated at Glenlivet by the Earls of Huntly and Erroll in 1594. His son, 'Cross-eyed Archibald', was a leader of the Covenanters. He was created a marquis in 1641, but in spite of his loyalty was beheaded in 1661. In 1685, his son Archibald was also beheaded, for his part in the Monmouth rebellion. Archibald, 10th Earl, returned with William of Orange, and was elevated by him to the dukedom. John, 9th Duke, married Princess Louise, daughter of Queen Victoria.

Campbell of Breadalbane

Crest Badge: *A boar's head, erased, proper.*

Motto: *Follow me.*

Gaelic Name: *Caimbeul.*

The Campbells of Breadalbane trace their family back to Sir Colin, son of Sir Duncan Campbell of Lochow. From his father he received the lands of Glenorchy, and through his marriage with a daughter of Lord Lorn he received a third part of the lands of Lorn. He built Kilchurn Castle in 1440, and for his valour on crusade in Palestine he was made a Knight of Rhodes.

The descendants of Sir Duncan were successful in adding to the possessions of the family, and in course of time these included the lands of Glenlyon, Finlarig, and territory throughout Argyll and Perthshire.

Sir John Campbell, 11th of Glenorchy, was created Earl of Breadalbane in 1681 and was a strong supporter of Charles II. He was described as being 'as cunning as a fox, as wise as a serpent, and as slippery as an eel'. Despite Jacobite leanings, in 1689 he was employed to bribe the Highland clans to submit to William III, a move which culminated in 1692 in the massacre of Glencoe, for which he was blamed. He died in 1716.

John, 14th of Breadalbane, was created a Baron of the United Kingdom in 1806 and raised to a marquessate in 1831. In 1862 the United Kingdom titles became extinct but the marquessate was restored to Gavin, 7th Earl, in 1885. On his death without issue, the marquessate again became extinct, but the Scottish honours devolved upon his nephew.

Campbell of Cawdor

Crest Badge: *A swan, proper, crowned, or.*

Motto: *Be mindful.*

Gaelic Name: *Caimbeul.*

The founder of this branch of the Clan Campbell was Sir John Campbell, third son of the 2nd Earl of Argyll, who married Muriella, daughter of Sir John Calder of Calder, in 1510. Sir John died in 1546, but his widow survived him by almost thirty years. On her death, the Thanedom of Cawdor passed to her grandson, John, who sold part of his estates in order to purchase the island of Islay, which remained in the possession of the Cawdor family until 1726 when it was purchased by Campbell of Shawfield.

Sir John, 8th of Cawdor, who married Mary, daughter of Lewis Pryce, died in 1777 and was succeeded by Pryce Campbell, member of parliament for Cromarty and Nairn. John, his son, was born in Scotland but spent most of his life in Wales. He was created Lord Cawdor of Castlemartin in Pembrokeshire in 1796. In the following year, when 1,200 French soldiers landed at Fishguard, the last foreign invasion of Great Britain, Lord Cawdor with a few troops and a large number of local people took them prisoner. He died in 1821 and was succeeded by his son, John Frederick Campbell, 2nd Baron, who was created Earl of Cawdor in 1827. Cawdor Castle, near Nairn, built about 1454, is one of the finest old castles in Scotland and is the residence of the chief.

Chisholm

Crest Badge: *A dexter hand couped at the wrist holding erect a dagger, proper, on which is transfixed a boar's head, couped, proper langued azure.*

Motto: *Feros ferio (I am fierce with the fierce).*

Gaelic Name: *Siosal.*

A chief of the clan once claimed that only three people in the world were entitled to use the definite article: 'The Pope, The King and The Chisholm'. It is claimed by some that the Chisholms are of Celtic origin; others claim that the clan came from the Borders and are of Norman origin. Sir Robert Gordon designates as Chisholm the Thane of Caithness who lived in the latter part of the 12th century. In the Ragman Rolls of 1296 mention is made of Richard de Cheschelme and John de Cheshome as having given allegiance to Edward I of England. In 1359 Sir Robert, Lord of Chisholm, succeeded his father-in-law as Constable of Urquhart Castle on Loch Ness. His son, Alexander, married the heiress of Erchless in Kintail and founded the family of Erchless and Strathglass. This family ceased in the male line, and in 1513 Wiland de Chesholm, of another branch, obtained the lands of Erchless.

In 1715 the clan served in the Jacobite cause under the Earl of Mar, and in 1745 the chief with his clan joined Prince Charles. They fought with great valour at Culloden, and during the Prince's wanderings after the battle, a Chisholm was one of the seven men who sheltered him in Glenmoriston, and afterwards led him across the country to Arisaig. Following The Chisholm's death in 1887, the chiefship passed to the descendants of the heiress of the senior direct line.

Clan Chattan

Crest Badge: *A cat salient.*

Motto: *Touch not the cat but a glove. (Touch not the cat without a glove).*

Gaelic Name: *Clann Gillacatan.*

Clan Chattan, or the 'Clan of the Cats', was a very ancient federation of clans. Originally made up of the Mackintoshes, Davidsons, Macphersons, MacGillivrays and MacBeans, it was later strengthened by the addition of other clans including the Farquharsons.

Gillechattan Mor is claimed to have been the first authentic chief, and from him descended Eva, only child of Dougall Dall, 6th chief. Her father conferred on Eva the chiefship, and when, in 1291, she married Angus, 6th Laird of Mackintosh, he became Captain of Clan Chattan as well.

The chiefs of Clan Macpherson also claimed the chiefship of Clan Chattan through descent from Muireach, the Parson of Kingussie in 1173, the father of Gilliechattan Mor and of Ewan Ban, progenitor of Clan Macpherson.

The feud between the two clans over the chiefship lasted for over two hundred yaers, the only gain by the Macphersons being the right of arms of a cadet of Clan Chattan. This position held until 1938 when the 28th chief of Mackintosh died without male issue. He had nominated his successor as chief of Clan Mackintosh but not of Clan Chattan so the chiefships of the two clan separated. It was not until 1947 that Duncan Alexander Elliot Mackintosh, descendant of the Daviot branch of the Mackintoshes, was granted the arms of Clan Chattan by the Lord Lyon.

Colquhoun

Crest Badge: *A hart's head, couped,*
gules, attired, argent.

Motto: *Si je puis (If I can).*

Gaelic Name: *Mac a' Chombaich.*

This clan takes its name from the lands of Colquhoun in
Dunbartonshire. These lands were granted to Humphrey of
Kilpatrick by Malcolm, Earl of Lennox, in the time of
Alexander II. In the 14th century, Sir Robert Kilpatrick of
Colquhoun married the daughter of the Laird of Luss, and
since then the chief has been described as of Colquhoun and
Luss.

In the 16th and 17th centuries, the Colquhouns were one of
the clans responsible for the outlawing of the MacGregors.
About 1602, after a conference between the two clans, the
Colquhouns hoped to trap the MacGregors in Glenfruin. Their
intention was anticipated, however, by Alastair MacGregor of
Glenstrae, and after a bloody conflict the Colquhouns were
signally defeated and their chief killed. In revenge they made a
dramatic representation to James VI, and the Clan Gregor was
proscribed and the name forbidden under pain of death, a
punishment which lasted well into the next century.

Sir Humphrey, 18th chief, surrendered his baronetcy for a new
grant to himself and his daughter and his son-in-law, James
Grant of Pluscarden, with a condition preventing the clan
name and estates passing to the Grants of Grant. Because of
this provision, two Grants in succession had to resign the
estates which then passed to a younger son of James Grant,
from whom the present Luss family is descended.

Cumming

Crest Badge: *A lion rampant, or, holding in his dexter paw a dagger, proper.*

Motto: *Courage.*

Gaelic Name: *Cuimean.*

When Robert the Bruce secured the throne of Scotland he generally rewarded his friends at the expense of his enemies, and the family of Comyn was among those who lost land and titles. The Cummings, however, to use the modern spelling, remained numerous in the northeast of Scotland.

The Cummings of Culter traced their descent from Jardine Comyn, son of a 13th-century Earl of Buchan. The Cummings of Relugas appear in the 16th century, but it is the Cummings of Altyre who have occupied the principal position since the fall of the Comyns.

The first of the Cummings of Altyre was Ferquhard, son of Sir Richard Cumming, a 14th-century descendant of the Lords of Badenoch. During the 15th and 16th centuries the Cummings were actively engaged in public affairs. In 1594 Alexander Cumming of Altyre commanded a troop of horse in Huntly's army at the Battle of Glenlivet.

In 1657 Robert Cumming of Altyre married Lucy, daughter of Sir Ludovick Gordon of Gordonstown, and when the last Gordon of Gordonstown died, Alexander Cumming of Altyre, being his heir, assumed the name and arms of Gordon of Gordonstown, and was created a baronet in 1804. He died in 1806, and his second son, Sir William, became 2nd Baronet. He was succeeded by his son Sir Alexander Penrose Gordon-Cumming whose brother Roualeyn was a famous 19th-century traveller and lion hunter.

Cunningham

Crest Badge: *A unicorn's head, argent, crined and armed, or.*

Motto: *Over fork over.*

Gaelic Name: *MacCuinneagain.*

The name of Cunningham occurs as early as the 12th century and is derived from the district of Cunninghame in Ayrshire. For his bravery at the Battle of Largs in 1263, Hervey de Cunningham received from Alexander III the lands of Kilmaurs. The Kilmaurs remained the principal family, and Sir William Cunningham, by his marriage to Margaret, daughter of Sir Robert Dennieston of that ilk, added many lands to his family possessions including Glencairn, from which Alexander de Cunningham took his title when created Earl of Glencairn by James III in 1488. He was killed at the Battle of Sauchieburn in the same year.

William Cunningham, 8th Earl of Glencairn, born about 1610, was a Privy Councillor, Commissioner of the Treasury in 1641, and Lord Justice General in 1646. In 1653 he raised an army in the Highlands in support of Charles II. After the Restoration he was appointed Lord Chancellor of Scotland. He died in 1664. James, 14th Earl, was a friend of Robert Burns, and when he died in 1791, Burns wrote his well-known 'Lament for the Earl of Glencairn'. With the death of John, 15th Earl, who died without issue in 1796, the earldom became dormant.

Many important branches of the family spread all over Scotland. The Cunninghams of Corsehill derive from the second son of the 3rd Earl of Glencairn. The Cunninghams of Caprington trace their ancestry back to the 14th century.

Davidson

Crest Badge: *A stag's head, erased, proper.*

Motto: *Sapienter si sincere (Wisely if sincerely).*

Gaelic Name: *MacDhaibhidh.*

Before 1350, Donald Dubh of Invernahaven, chief of the Davidsons, having married the daughter of Angus, 6th of Mackintosh, sought the protection of his brother-in-law William, 7th of Mackintosh, and thus became associated with the Clan Chattan confederation.

The clan is known as Clann Dhai from its first chief, David Dubh of Invernahaven, and it is clear that its entry into Clan Chattan led to some dispute, probably as to precedence. Enmity was particularly marked between the Davidsons and the Macphersons. In 1370, when the Mackintosh headed several branches of the Clan Chattan in a battle with the Camerons on the matter of conflicting claims to lands in Lochaber, the Macphersons dissociated themselves from the confederation and watched its defeat. During the night, Mackintosh sent his bard, as coming from the Camerons, to the camp of the Macphersons and accused them of cowardice. Thus enraged, the Macphersons attacked the Camerons and completely defeated them.

The dispute between the two branches was of long standing, and some authorities name the Clann Dhai as the group opposing the Macphersons at the Battle of the North Inch of Perth, in 1396.

In the 18th century we find important families like the Davidsons of Cantray and the Davidsons of Tulloch, the latter family coming into possession of the lands and castle of Tulloch, near Dingwall.

Douglas

Crest Badge: *On a chapeau a salamander, vert, in fire, proper.*

Motto: *Jamais arrière (Never behind).*

Gaelic Name: *Dubhghlas.*

Although this was one of the most powerful families in Scotland, its origins are unknown. The first bearer of the name was William de Duglas, who is on record between 1175 and 1199. He had six sons, five associated with the Province of Moray.

The Douglases were prominent in the struggle for Scotland's independence in the days of Wallace and Bruce, and 'the Good Sir James', while carrying Bruce's heart to the Holy Land, was killed fighting against the Moors in Spain in 1330. His nephew, William, was created Earl of Douglas in 1357, and became Earl of Mar by his marriage with Margaret, sister of the 13th Earl of Mar. James, 2nd Earl of this line, from whom descended the Queensbury branch, was killed at Otterburn in 1388. James's half-brother George became Earl of Angus. The earldom of Douglas was forfeited in 1455 when James, 9th Earl, deserted the Scottish cause.

George Douglas obtained the earldom of Angus in 1389 when his mother resigned it in his favour. He married Mary, daughter of Robert III. Archibald, 6th Earl, was for a long period in rebellion against James V, and kept the young king a prisoner for over three years. William, 11th Earl of Angus, was created Marquis of Douglas in 1633.

Archibald, 3rd Marquis, was created Duke of Douglas in 1703. He died without heir in 1761, and his titles, except the dukedom, passed to the 7th Duke of Hamilton.

Drummond

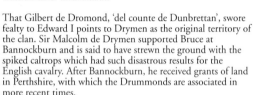

Crest Badge: *Out of crest coronet a goshawk, wings expanded, proper, jessed gules.*

Motto: *Gang warily (Go carefully).*

Gaelic Name: *Drummann.*

That Gilbert de Dromond, 'del counte de Dunbrettan', swore fealty to Edward I points to Drymen as the original territory of the clan. Sir Malcolm de Drymen supported Bruce at Bannockburn and is said to have strewn the ground with the spiked caltrops which had such disastrous results for the English cavalry. After Bannockburn, he received grants of land in Perthshire, with which the Drummonds are associated in more recent times.

Margaret Drummond married David II in 1369, and Annabella Drummond, who married Robert III, was the mother of James I.

Sir John Drummond was created Lord Drummond in 1488, and in 1605 James VI conferred the earldom of Perth on the 4th Baron Drummond.

The Drummonds were loyal to the Stuarts and received honours such as the earldom of Melfort and the viscountcy of Strathallan. During the Jacobite Risings, the Earl of Perth was created a Duke by James VII after his escape to France, and in 1745 the clan followed Prince Charles. Viscount Strathallan died at Culloden, while the Duke of Perth escaped to France. The Drummond estates were forfeited, but were restored in 1785 to the great-grandson of the first Earl, who became Lord Perth in 1797. Descent through the French line then followed, the earldom of Perth and chiefship of Clan Drummond finally passing to the Strathallan line.

Duncan

Crest Badge: *A ship under sail.*

Motto: *Disce pati (Learn to suffer).*

Gaelic Name: *Mac Dhonnchaidh.*

The Duncans and the Robertsons, or Clann Donnachaidh, appear to have had the same origin. They were descended from the ancient Earls of Atholl and took their name from the chief Donnachadh Reamhar, or 'Fat Duncan', who led the clan at the Battle of Bannockburn.

The Duncans possessed lands in old Forfarshire, modern Angus, including the barony of Lundie and the estate of Gourdie. Sir William Duncan was one of the physicians to George III, and in 1764 was created a baronet, but the title became extinct on his death in 1774.

Alexander Duncan of Lundie, provost of Dundee, was a royalist during the Jacobite Rising of 1745. He married Helena, daughter of Haldane of Gleneagles, and their second son, Adam, born in 1731, entered the navy in 1746, and in 1780 he defeated the Spanish at Cape St Vincent. In 1795 he was appointed commander of the fleet in the North Sea and Admiral of the Blue. He had blockaded the Dutch fleet for two years when the mutiny at the Spithead and Nore spread to all his own ships except the Venerable, his flagship, and the Adamant. By a stratagem he kept the Dutch in the Texel, and in 1797 he gained at Camperdown one of the most glorious victories in the history of the British Navy. For his services he was created Viscount Duncan of Camperdown by George IV in 1800.

Elliot

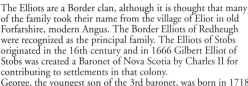

Crest Badge: *A dexter cubit arm in armour, erect, in hand a broadsword, proper.*

Motto: *Fortiter et recte*
(With strength and right).

Old Motto: *Soyez sage (Be wise).*

The Elliots are a Border clan, although it is thought that many of the family took their name from the village of Eliot in old Forfarshire, modern Angus. The Border Elliots of Redheugh were recognized as the principal family. The Elliots of Stobs originated in the 16th century and in 1666 Gilbert Elliot of Stobs was created a Baronet of Nova Scotia by Charles II for contributing to settlements in that colony.

George, the youngest son of the 3rd baronet, was born in 1718. He entered the army and served in the War of the Austrian Succession. He was Governor of Gibraltar when, in 1779, Spain and France laid siege to that important fortress. Over 100,000 men, 48 ships and 450 cannon were used by the enemy, but the British under Elliot remained undefeated. When Lord Howe relieved Gibraltar, the loss of the garrison in nine weeks was 65 dead and 388 wounded. Elliot was created Lord Heathfield, Baron Gibraltar, in 1787.

Gilbert Elliot, descended from the Stobs branch, was the founder of the Minto family. Born in 1651 he followed the profession of the Law. His work for religious liberty led to his being condemned for high treason in 1685. He was pardoned, and was constituted a Lord of Session as Lord Minto in 1705. His great-grandson, Gilbert, was Governor General of India from 1807 until 1812, and was created Earl of Minto in 1813.

Erskine

Crest Badge: *Out of cap of maintenance gules turned ermine, a dexter hand holding a dagger in pale proper.*

Motto: *Je pense plus (I think more).*

Gaelic Name: *Arascain.*

This ancient name is derived from the barony of Erskine in Renfrewshire, which was owned by Henry of Erskine in the 13th century. The family were loyal adherents of Robert the Bruce, to whom they were related by marriage. Sir Robert de Erskine was Great Chamberlain of Scotland, and constable and keeper of the castles of Stirling, Edinburgh and Dumbarton. He died in 1385.

Sir Robert Erskine assumed the old Celtic title of Earl of Mar in 1435. His son, Sir Thomas, was dispossessed of it by James II in 1457, but in 1467 he was created Lord Erskine. John, 4th Lord Erskine, had charge of the infant Mary Queen of Scots in Stirling Castle and Inchmahome, and took her to France. His son, Alexander, was ancestor of the Earls of Kellie. In 1565, John, 5th Lord Erskine, was confirmed in the earldom of Mar by Mary Queen of Scots but it was forfeited in 1716 by the 11th Earl, a leader of the Jacobite Rising of 1715, and restored in 1824. James Erskine, son of the 7th Earl of Mar, acquired the earldom of Buchan by his marriage to the Countess of Buchan.

The Erskines of Dun descended from the Erskines of Erskine when Sir Thomas received a charter of the Barony of Dun from Robert II in 1376. Many of the family of Dun fell at Flodden in 1513, and the estate of Dun eventually passed to the Marquis of Ailsa in 1793. His second son inherited the property and assumed the name Erskine.

Farquharson

Crest Badge: *Out of chapeau gules turned ermine a demi-lion rampant, gules, holding in his dexter paw a sword, proper pommelled, or.*

Motto: *Fide et fortitudine*
(By fidelity and fortitude).

Gaelic Name: *MacFhearchair.*

This Aberdeenshire clan was a member of the Clan Chattan confederation, and took its name from Farquhar, son of Shaw of Rothiemurchus.

A prominent member of the clan was Finlay Mor, who carried the royal standard at the Battle of Pinkie where he was killed in 1547. In 1639 the Farquharsons of Monaltrie joined Lord Gordon on the royalist side and six years later they formed part of the army of Montrose. They fought at the Battle of Worcester in 1651, and followed Viscount Dundee. In 1715 they formed part of the Clan Chattan who fought and were defeated at Preston. In 1745 they formed part of the Jacobite army, and distinguished themselves at Falkirk and Culloden. Francis of Monaltrie, known as the Baron Ban, was taken prisoner at Culloden. He was reprieved and allowed to reside in England. He returned to Scotland in 1766.

The Farquharsons acquired Invercauld by marriage with the MacHardy heiress of Invercauld. In 1595 the Farquharsons acknowledged Mackintosh as their chief in a document signed at Invercauld. The Farquharsons of Invercauld were out in the Jacobite cause in 1715 and in 1745. Anne Farquharson, known as 'Colonel Anne', who had married Angus, 22nd chief of the clan Mackintosh, raised the Mackintoshes for Prince Charles, while her husband fought on the side of Hanover.

Fergus(s)on

Crest Badge: *A bee on a thistle all proper.*

Motto: *Dulcius ex asperis*
(Sweeter after difficulties).

Gaelic Name: *MacFhearghuis.*

Many families of this name were established throughout Scotland by an early date. In Perthshire there were the Fergusons of Dunfallandy and Balquhidder, in Aberdeenshire the families of Kinmundy and Pitfour, in Fife the Fergusons of Raith, in Ayrshire the Kilkerran family, and in Dumfriesshire the Fergussons of Craigdarroch who claim descent from Fergus, Prince of Galloway in the 12th century, and whose family lands have been in their possession since the 15th century.

In Argyll, where the clan is numerous, the Fergusons held lands in Strachur until the beginning of the 19th century, and there appears to be a connection between them and the Fergussons of Kilkerran. The Kilkerran family was active in affairs of state, and Sir James, 2nd Baronet, was appointed Lord of Session in 1735, when he took the title of Lord Kilkerran. His son George, Lord of Session in 1799, took the title Lord Hermand. The Fergusons acquired the estate of Raith in Fife in the early 19th century, and one of its members was General Sir Ronald C. Ferguson, Colonel of the Cameron Highlanders, who received a special medal from George III for his services in Portugal.

The Fergussons of Perthshire were recognized as the principal Highland branch of the clan, with the chieftainship in the Dunfallandy family, the head of which was designated MacFhearghuis, 'son of Fergus'.

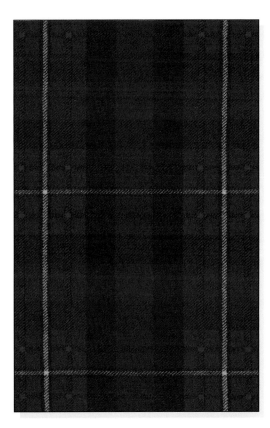

Fletcher

Crest Badge: *Two naked arms proper shooting an arrow out of a bow sable.*

Gaelic Name: *Mac an Fhleisteir*

A fletcher is a maker of arrows, and the name is therefore associated with many clans, among them the Stewarts and the Campbells in Argyll and the MacGregors in Perthshire. For recovering cattle stolen by the MacDonalds in 1497, Stewart of Appin agreed to help the Fletchers when they required assistance, but about a century later the Fletchers and the Campbells of Glenorchy entered into a bond. The Fletchers claim to have been the original inhabitants in Glenorchy in Argyll, and a local saying runs, 'It was the clan Fletcher that raised the first smoke to boil water in Orchy'.

The Fletchers of Glenlyon followed the MacGregors, for whom they were arrow-makers, and it is on record that a Fletcher once saved the life of Rob Roy. The Fletchers were also out in the Rising of 1745.

In 1643, the Fletchers of Innerpeffer in Angus purchased the estate of Saltoun in Haddington. To this family belonged Andrew Fletcher, the celebrated Scottish patriot, and his nephew, another Andrew, who became a distinguished judge, Lord Milton.

Archibald Fletcher, styled the father of burgh reform, was born in Glenlyon in 1745, son of Angus Fletcher, a younger brother of Archibald Fletcher of Bennice and Dunans. The Fletchers of Dunans was an important family during the 18th and 19th centuries.

In later years the name Fletcher became confused with that of Flesher, so that many Fletchers may be Fleshers and vice versa.

Forbes

Crest Badge: *A stag's head, proper.*

Motto: *Grace me guide.*

Gaelic Name: *Foirbeis.*

This clan traces its origin to John of Forbes who held the lands of Forbes in Aberdeenshire in the 13th century. In 1303 Alexander of Forbes was killed during the attack on Urquhart Castle on Loch Ness by English troops, and his son was killed at the Battle of Dupplin near Perth in 1332. Alexander Forbes was created a peer by James II in 1442, as Baron Forbes, and he married the grand-daughter of Robert III.

The Forbes' of Culloden were descended from Sir John Forbes of Forbes through the Forbes of Tolquhoun. Duncan Forbes, the Laird of Culloden, who was Lord President of the Court of Session at the time of the 1745 Rising, exercised his powerful influence to prevent many of the clans from joining the army of Prince Charles. It is possible that, had the government been willing to listen to his advice, the Rising might never have happened. George II proved an ungrateful sovereign, and Forbes received no reward for his loyalty.

The peerage of Pitsligo was conferred on Alexander Forbes in 1633. Alexander, 4th Lord Pitsligo, protested against the Union of 1707 and took part in the Jacobite Risings of 1715 and 1745. His estates were forfeited, and on the death of his son the title became dormant. The Forbes' of Craigievar were descended from James, 2nd Lord Forbes. Sir William, 8th of Craigievar, succeeded his cousin as Lord Sempill, Premier Baron of Scotland.

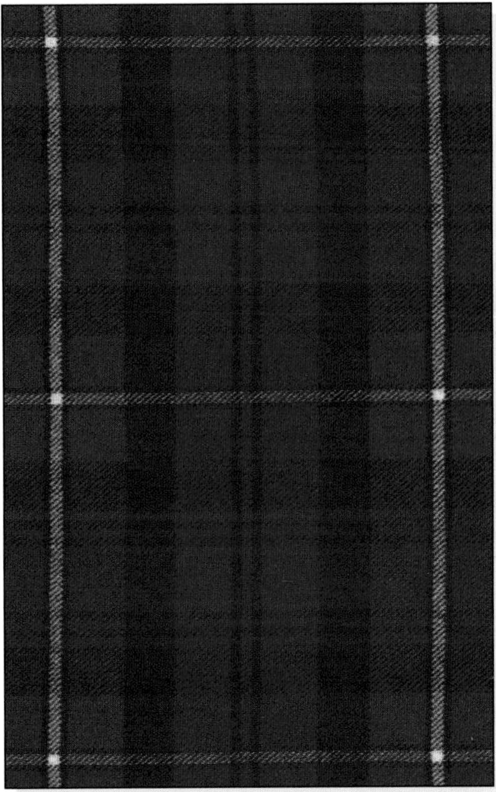

Fraser of Lovat

Crest Badge: *A buck's head, erased, or tyned argent.*

Motto: *Je suis prest (I am ready).*

Gaelic Name: *Friseal.*

The name of Fraser, said to be of Norman origin, is first found in the south of Scotland in the 12th century. The first recorded Fraser in the Highlands was possibly Sir Andrew Fraser who acquired the lands of Lovat through his wife, the daughter of the Earl of Orkney and Caithness.

In 1544 the Frasers supported the claim of Ranald, who had been fostered by Lovat, to the chiefship of Clan Ranald, against that of John MacDonald of Moidart. As a result, the Battle of the Shirts was fought on the shores of Loch Lochy between the two clans with such determination that only five Frasers and eight MacDonalds remained alive.

In the royalist cause, the Frasers opposed Montrose but supported Viscount Dundee. Simon Fraser, 11th Lord Lovat, the Old Fox, supported the government in the 1715 Rising but switched to the Jacobite cause in 1745. For the clan's part, Lord Lovat was executed, although it was his son who had commanded the clan at Culloden. The son was pardoned for his part, and in 1757 raised 1,800 Frasers for service in America.

Because of the Jacobite activity, the title was attainted in 1747, and about fifty years later the direct line failed. In 1837 Thomas of Strichen was created Baron Lovat, and from him is descended the present Lord Lovat. Lady Saltoun is chief of Clan Fraser, but the Frasers of Lovat have for long formed the Highland branch.

Gordon

Crest Badge: *Out of crest coronet a buck's head cabossed, proper, attired or.*

Motto: *Bydand (Remaining).*

Gaelic Name: *Gôrdon.*

The Gordons came from the Lowlands to Aberdeenshire in the 14th century when Sir Adam, Lord of Gordon, was granted lands in Strathbogie by Robert the Bruce. Elizabeth, only child of a later Adam Gordon, married Alexander Seton who assumed the name of Gordon, and their son was created Earl of Huntly in 1449. A marquessate was conferred on the 6th Earl in 1599, and a dukedom on the 4th Marquess by Charles II in 1684. The titles died with the 5th Duke, the marquessate going to the Earl of Aboyne and the estates to the Duke of Richmond who, in 1876, was created Duke of Gordon.

The Gordons of Methlic acquired the lands of Haddo in 1533, and in 1642 Sir John was created a baronet of Nova Scotia by Charles I. Sir George, who was President of the Court of Session, received the earldom of Aberdeen in 1682, and John, 7th Earl and 1st Marquess, was Governor-General of Canada and later Lord-Lieutenant of Ireland.

The Gordons of Kirkcudbright were descended from the original stem of Border Gordons and in the 14th century acquired the lands of Lochinvar and Kenmure. In 1633 Sir John Gordon was created Viscount Kenmure and Lord Lochinvar. They were strong supporters of the Stuarts, and the 6th Viscount was executed after the 1715 Rising, and his estates forfeited.

The regiment, later known as the Gordon Highlanders, was first raised in 1794, with the assistance of Jane, Duchess of Gordon.

Gow or MacGowan

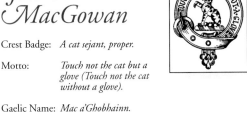

Crest Badge: *A cat sejant, proper.*

Motto: *Touch not the cat but a glove (Touch not the cat without a glove).*

Gaelic Name: *Mac a'Ghobhainn.*

The name Gow is derived from the Gaelic word Gobha meaning a blacksmith or armourer, but it may be a shortening of Mac a'Ghobhainn (MacGowan), 'son of the smith'.

The names Gow and MacGowan are associated with several clans - smiths being essential - but the main Highland branch is believed to be connected with the Macphersons and Clan Chattan. This connection is based on an incident said to have taken place at a clan conflict on the North Inch of Perth in 1396 when Henry Wynd, known as 'an gobh crom' (the crooked smith) - who was immortalized by Sir Walter Scott as 'Hal o' the Wynd' in The Fair Maid of Perth - took part in the conflict on behalf of one of the clans.

The Gows made their homes chiefly in the shires of Perth and Inverness, and amongst the notable bearers of the name were Neil Gow (1727-1807), the prince of Scottish fiddlers and composer of many popular reels and strathspeys, and his scarcely less celebrated son, Nathaniel (1766-1831).

Following the failure of the 1745 Rising, one Gow, John, took refuge in Glenlivet where he adopted the name Smith and earned his living by making whisky. The MacGowans appear to be widely scattered throughout Scotland, and in earlier times were found in Stirling, Glasgow, Fife, Dumfries, and in the Lowlands, and a clan MacGowan is said to have been located in or near Nithsdale in the 12th century.

Graham

Crest Badge: *A falcon wings displayed, proper, beaked and armed, or, preying on a stork on its back argent, armed gules.*

Motto: *Ne oublie (Do not forget).*

Gaelic Name: *Greumach.*

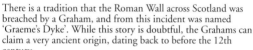

There is a tradition that the Roman Wall across Scotland was breached by a Graham, and from this incident was named 'Graeme's Dyke'. While this story is doubtful, the Grahams can claim a very ancient origin, dating back to before the 12th century.

The first of the name recorded in Scotland is William de Graham who received the lands of Abercorn and Dalkeith from David I. Sir John Graham of Dundaff, the 'richt hand' of Wallace, was killed at the Battle of Falkirk in 1298. The 3rd Lord Graham was created Earl of Montrose by James IV in 1504, and fell at Flodden in 1513. James, 5th Earl, was created Marquis of Montrose in 1644. He was a brilliant soldier, and his campaign in Scotland one of the most masterly in military annals. He was executed in Edinburgh in 1650. James, 4th Marquis, was elevated in 1707 to the dukedom of Montrose. It was to the Marquis of Graham, afterwards 3rd Duke of Montrose, that Highlanders owe the repeal, in 1782, of the Act of 1747 prohibiting the wearing of Highland dress.

Another famous soldier descended from the Montrose family was John Graham of Claverhouse, Viscount Dundee. During his campaign against the Covenanters he gained the name 'Bloody Clavers', but to his supporters and to his friends he was affectionately known as 'Bonnie Dundee'. He died in his hour of triumph at the Battle of Killiecrankie in 1689.

Grant

Crest Badge: *A mountain inflamed, proper.*

Motto: *Stand fast.*

Gaelic Name: *Grannd.*

The Clan Grant is one of the clans claiming to belong to Siol Alpine and to be descended from Kenneth MacAlpine, the 9th-century king of Scotland.

In the 13th century the Grants appear as Sheriffs of Inverness. They exerted considerable influence in the northeast of Scotland and supported Wallace in his struggle. John Grant, chief of the clan, married the daughter of Gilbert of Glencairnie, and from his elder son sprang the Grants of Freuchie. His younger son was progenitor of the Tullochgorm branch of the clan. From John Grant of Freuchie are descended the Earls of Seafield, the Grants of Corrimony and the Grants of Glenmoriston.

The Grants were consistently royalists and in 1690 took part in the notable battle on the Haughs of Cromdale which gave its name to the famous pipe tune. In the Jacobite Risings the clan supported the Hanoverian side, although the Grants of Glenmoriston supported the Jacobite cause.

Ludovic Grant of Grant, the then chief, married for his second wife Lady Margaret Ogilvie, daughter of the Earl of Findlater and Seafield, and his grandson succeeded to the Seafield peerage. The 8th Earl died without issue and the titles passed to his uncle, James, 9th Earl of Seafield. The 11th Earl of Seafield was killed in the First World War, and the Ogilvie honours passed to his only child, Nina, Countess of Seafield. The chiefship of Clan Grant remained in the Lords Strathspey.

Gunn

Crest Badge: *A dexter hand holding a sword in bend all proper.*

Motto: *Aut pax aut bellum (Either peace or war).*

Gaelic Name: *Guinne.*

The territory of the Clan Gunn was in Caithness and Sutherland, and the clan claim to be descended from Olave the Black, Norse king of Man and the Isles, who died in 1237. True to their name, which means 'battle', the clan were noted for their warlike and ferocious character and continued to extend their possessions until the 15th century, but their continual feuds with other clans led to their settling, at a later date, chiefly in Sutherland.

A chief of the clan who flourished in the 15th century was George Gunn, who held the office of Crowner, the badge of which was a great brooch. He lived in magnificent style in his castle at Clyth, but was killed by treachery in 1464 when endeavouring to arrange a reconciliation with the Clan Keith, between whom and the Gunns there had been a continuing feud. The Crowner was one of the greatest men in the country at that time, and his death was avenged about a century later by his grandson, who killed Keith of Ackergill, his son and twelve followers at Drummoy in Sutherland.

Feuds continued between the Gunns and the Mackays, and the Earls of Caithness and Sutherland, and in 1585 the Earls attacked the Gunns who, although fewer in number, held the advantage of a position on higher ground. The Gunns killed 140 of their enemies, and only darkness prevented a great slaughter. The Gunns, however, were later defeated at Lochbroom by the Earl of Sutherland.

Hamilton

Crest Badge: *On a ducal coronet an oak tree fructed and penetrated transversely in the main by a frame saw, proper, the frame or.*

Motto: *Through.*

Gaelic Name: *Hamultun.*

The name probably comes from Leicestershire, and the first record of it in Scotland is claimed for Walter Fitz-Gilbert from whom are descended the Dukes of Hamilton. Walter witnessed a charter in 1294 conferring on the monastery of Paisley the privilege of herring fishing in the Clyde. He was Governor of Bothwell Castle for the English during part of the Scottish War of Independence, but later joined Robert the Bruce from whom he received the Barony of Cadzow.

James, 6th of Cadzow, created Lord Hamilton in 1445, married Princess Mary, eldest daughter of James II and widow of the Earl of Arran. James, his son, was created Earl of Arran in 1503 and Duke of Chatelherault in France in 1549. His second son was created Marquis of Hamilton in 1599 and his fourth son was the ancestor of the Earls of Abercorn. James, 3rd Marquis, was created Duke of Hamilton in 1643. The 2nd Duke, William, died from wounds received at the Battle of Worcester in 1651 and was succeeded by his niece Anne, Duchess of Hamilton, who married Lord William Douglas, through whom the Hamilton titles passed to the Douglas family.

James Hamilton, grandson of the 2nd Earl of Arran, was created Earl of Abercorn in 1603, and in 1790 a marquessate was conferred on the 9th Earl whose son, the 2nd Marquess, was elevated to a dukedom in 1868.

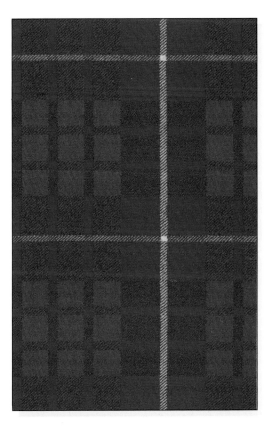

Hay

Crest Badge: *Out of a crest coronet a falcon rising, proper, armed and beaked or, jessed, and belled or.*

Motto: *Serva jugum*
(Keep the yoke).

Gaelic Name: *Mac Garaidh.*

The Hays descend from William de la Haye who came to Scotland about 1160, married a Celtic heiress and received the lands of Erroll from William the Lion about 1180. His grandson, Gilbert, 3rd Baron of Erroll, was co-Regent of Scotland. Sir Gilbert, 5th chief, one of the heroes of the Scottish War of Independence, was given Slains Castle in Buchan and made hereditary Constable of Scotland by Bruce himself. Thomas, 7th chief, married Robert II's daughter, and William, 9th chief, was belted Earl of Erroll in 1452. William, 4th Earl, fell at Flodden with 87 Hays. Francis, 9th Earl, in alliance with Huntly defeated Argyll at Glenlivet in 1594, but James VI personally blew up Slains Castle because the Earl was plotting with his Spanish enemies. A new castle, sited a few miles farther north, was built in 1664.

In 1627, Sir George Hay, descended from a younger branch of the same stock as the Earl of Erroll, was made Viscount Dupplin and Lord Hay of Kingauns, and in 1633 was created Earl of Kinnoul. The 9th and 10th Earls of Kinnoul successively held the office of Lord Lyon from 1796 until 1866 when the office was put on a professional footing.

John Hay of Restalrigg, a cadet of Kinnoul, was for a while a close companion of the Old Pretender in exile and was created 1st Earl and then Duke of Inverness in the Jacobite peerage.

Henderson

Crest Badge: *A dexter hand holding a star argent surmounted by a crescent. or.*

Motto: *Sola virtus nobilitat (Virtue alone ennobles).*

Gaelic Name: *Mac Eanruig.*

The name Henderson in Gaelic is Mac Eanruig, sometimes rendered in English as MacKendrick, and is found in widely separated districts in Scotland. Those in Caithness and the north claim to be a sept of the Clan Gunn.

The principal family of Hendersons was the Clan Eanruig of Glencoe, for whom it is claimed that they were in that glen of grievous memory centuries before the MacIans, or MacDonalds, arrived there. Tradition states that 'Iain Fraoch', a brother of John, 1st Lord of the Isles, married a daughter of the chief of the Hendersons of Glencoe and that their son Iain was the founder of the MacIains of Glencoe. He was called 'Iain Abrach', from his being born in Lochaber, and the clan came to be known as the Clan Abrach. The Hendersons, who were notable for their strength, always formed the bodyguard of the chief and were the hereditary pipers of the Clan Abrach.

From the Hendersons of Fordell in Angus was descended the Reverend Alexander Henderson, who was prominent in the Presbyterian Church of Scotland during the early 17th century. He helped to prepare the National Covenant of 1638 and was Moderator of the Glasgow Assembly which outlined Presbyterian organisation in the same year. He drafted the Solemn League and Covenant in 1643 and was a member of the Westminster Assembly which issued the Confession of Faith.

Innes

Crest Badge: *A boar's head erased proper.*

Motto: *Be traist (Be faithful).*

Gaelic Name: *Innis.*

This clan is of ancient origin and is found in the province of Moray as early as the 12th century when Berowald, described as Flandrensis, 'Flemish', received a charter of the lands of Innes from Malcolm IV in 1160. His grandson assumed the name Innes from his lands and received confirmation of his charter from Alexander II in 1226. By marriage, Sir Alexander, 9th of Innes, acquired the lands of Aberchirder in the 14th century, and branches of the family established themselves all over the north of Scotland. Alexander, 13th of Innes, had large landed possessions and received many charters between the years 1493 and 1533. Robert, 20th of Innes, was created a baronet in 1625. Sir Harry, 4th Baronet, married a daughter of Duncan Forbes of Culloden.

In 1767, the 6th Baronet, Sir James, sold the lands of Innes to the Earl of Fife and went to reside in England, but on the death of the 4th Duke of Roxburghe, as heir-general he claimed the Scottish titles and estates of that family, and the House of Lords decided in his favour. He assumed the name Ker and succeeded as 5th Duke of Roxburghe. James, 6th Duke, was created Earl Innes in 1836.

Through the Inneses of Innermarkie, the family of Balveny are descended from the Inneses of that Ilk. Robert, 5th Baron of Innermarkie, acquired the lands of Balveny in Banffshire and was created a baronet in 1631.

Johnston

Crest Badge: *A winged spur or, leathered gules.*

Motto: *Nunquam non paratus (Never unprepared).*

Gaelic Name: *MacIain.*

The Johnstons were a powerful clan who derived their name from the barony of Johnston in Annandale. The name occurs in records of the 13th century, and from that time onward they were prominent in Border warfare. The Johnstons supported the Crown for generations, and in 1633 Sir James Johnston of Johnston was created Lord Johnston of Lochwood by Charles I and ten years later Earl of Hartfell. The extinct earldom of Annandale was conferred on the 2nd Earl of Hartfell who died in 1672. His son was created Marquess of Annandale in 1701. The marquessate became dormant on the death of George, 3rd Marquess, in 1792.

The Johnstons of Westerhall in Dumfriesshire were descended from the same stock, and John, 2nd of Westerhall, was created a Baronet of Nova Scotia in 1700.

The Johnstons of the north claim descent from Stiven de Johnston in the 14th century whose grandson possessed the lands of Ballindalloch. George Johnston of that Ilk was created a Baronet of Nova Scotia in 1626. Sir John, 3rd Baronet, was unjustly executed in London in 1690 for being present at the marriage of Captain Campbell of Mamore who was alleged to have abducted Miss Wharton and married her. Campbell escaped to Scotland, but Johnston was betrayed by his landlord for £50. Sir John, 4th Baronet, was out for the Jacobites in the 1745 Rising, and his son was killed at Sheriffmuir.

Keith

Crest Badge: *Out of crest coronet a stag's head erased, proper, attired with tynes or.*

Motto: *Veritas vincit*
(Truth conquers).

Gaelic Name: *Ceiteach.*

One of the most powerful Celtic families, the Keiths held the office of Great Marischal from the 12th century. In the 14th century they took possession, through marriage, of lands in Caithness, and for a long time their settlement there was a source of feuds with the Clan Gunn. An attempt at reconciliation being unsuccessful, a meeting was arranged between twelve horsemen from both sides. The Keiths arrived with two men on each horse and attacked the Gunns while they were at prayer. Both sides fought with desperation until most of the Gunns were killed, including their chief, and the Keiths retired considerably depleted. The surviving Gunns later followed and killed many of the remaining Keiths.

Sir William Keith was created Earl Marischal by James II in 1458, and the family exerted considerable influence in Scotland for centuries afterwards. George, 5th Earl Marischal, founded Marischal College in Aberdeen University. James, younger son of the 9th Earl Marischal and brother of the 10th, was a notable soldier, who was out in the Jacobite Rising of 1715. He joined the Russian army in 1728 and became a General in 1737. Ten years later he joined the German army and was made a Field-Marshal by Frederick the Great. On the death of George, last Earl Marischal in 1778, the entailed estates passed to Lord Falconer, and the remainder of his property was divided among his grand-nephews.

Kennedy

Crest Badge: *A dolphin naiant, proper.*

Motto: *Avise la fin*
(Consider the end).

Gaelic Name: *MacUalraig,*
Ceannaideach.

This ancient clan, whose name means 'ugly head', is found associated with the southwest of Scotland from the 12th century, and the history of the Carrick district of Ayrshire is substantially the early history of the Kennedys. They are claimed to have descended from the 1st Earl of Carrick. The Kennedys of Dunure acquired Cassillis, and later one of the family married Mary, daughter of Robert III. Their son was created Lord Kennedy in 1457, and in 1509 the 3rd Lord was created Earl of Cassilis. Gilbert, 4th Earl, earned an infamous reputation for his dreadful deed of 'roasting the Abbot of Crossraguel' in the black vault of Dunure Castle to obtain possession of the lands of the Abbey. The 6th Earl raised a regiment which suffered heavily in the defeats of Alford and Kilsyth in the Covenanting struggle. Archibald, 12th Earl of Cassillis, was created Baron Ailsa in 1806, and in 1831 Marquess of Ailsa. Culzean Castle was built between 1775 and 1790 by the 9th and 10th Earls. It was designed by Robert Adam.

Tradition tells that Ulric Kennedy fled from Ayrshire for some lawless deed and settled in Lochaber where his descendants were known as Clan Ulric. The Kennedys of Skye, and other districts of the Highlands, trace their descent from this branch of the family. The Lochaber Kennedys joined forces with the Camerons and are accepted as a sept of that clan.

Kerr

Crest Badge: *The sun in his splendour.*

Motto: *Sero sed serio*
(Late but in earnest).

Gaelic Name: *Cearr, MacGhillechearr.*

Traditionally the Kerrs are of Anglo-Norman origin, descended from two brothers who settled in Roxburgh in the 14th century, although the name may have existed in the 12th century, and it is also claimed that the name comes from a Celtic word meaning strength.

The Kers of Cessford were Wardens of the Marches and prominent in Border conflicts. They were granted old Roxburgh by James IV, and Sir Walter Cessford fought on the side of James VI at Langside in 1568. Sir Robert, born in 1570, was created Lord Roxburghe in 1600, and in 1616 was elevated to the earldom of Roxburghe and appointed Lord Privy Seal in 1637. By marriage with the Earl's daughter Jean, Sir William Drummond became 2nd Earl of Roxburghe and assumed the name Ker. John, 5th Earl, supported the Union of 1707 and was created Duke of Roxburghe. The direct line failed on the death of the 3rd Duke. Lord Bellenden became 4th Duke and his death without surviving issue led to a long and confused contest. Sir James Innes succeeded as 5th Duke and assumed the name Ker.

In 1606 Mark Ker of Newbattle was created Earl of Lothian. His son Robert, 2nd Earl, had no male issue, and the title passed through his daughter to her husband, William Kerr, son of the 1st Earl of Ancrum, who became 3rd Earl of Lothian in 1631. Robert, 4th Earl, was raised to the marquessate of Lothian in 1701.

Lamont

Crest Badge: *A dexter hand, open, pale-ways, couped at the wrist, proper.*

Motto: *Ne parcas nec spernas (Neither spare nor dispose).*

Gaelic Name: *MacLaomainn.*

The Clan Lamont, whose Norse name means 'law-giver', is of great antiquity and once held considerable lands in Argyll, which were later reduced by the encroachment of the Campbells and others until they were confined chiefly to Cowal.

In the early 13th century Laumun granted to the monks of Paisley certain lands at Kilmun and Kilfinan, and in 1456 John Lamont was Bailie of Cowal. John Lamont of Inveryne was knighted in 1539 and had his lands united into the Barony of Inveryne. At this time his principal seat was at Toward Castle, where he entertained Mary Queen of Scots in 1563.

During the disturbed period of the Civil War, several of the Campbell chiefs ravaged the Lamont country with fire and sword, destroying Toward and Ascog Castles, and in 1646 treacherously massacred two hundred Lamonts at Dunoon. The massacre formed one of the charges against the Marquess of Argyll, for which he was executed in 1661. After the destruction of Toward Castle, Ardlamont became the principal residence of the chief. The family were connected by marriage to many of the titled families of Scotland. John, 19th chief, commanded the Gordon Highlanders at Corunna in 1809. One of the oldest cadet families, and the only one still possessing the old clan lands, is the Lamonts of Knockdow.

Leslie

Crest Badge: *A demi-griffin, proper.*

Motto: *Grip fast.*

The family takes its name from the lands of Leslie in Aberdeenshire. In the 12th century Bartholomew, a Flemish noble, obtained the Barony of Lesly, and from him are descended the Earls of Rothes, the title being conferred on George de Lesly of Rothes. His grandson, George, 2nd Earl, was killed at Flodden. The Leslies were concerned in the murder of Cardinal Beaton, and George, 4th Earl, was tried for his part in it but acquitted. Andrew, 5th Earl, who succeeded his father in 1588, was a supporter of Mary Queen of Scots. John, 6th Earl, was a powerful leader of the Covenanters. John, 7th Earl, was created Duke of Rothes in 1680, but as he died without male issue the dukedom died with him. The earldom continued through his daughter.

General Alexander Leslie of the Balgonie family served under Gustavus Adolphus, King of Sweden, and rose to be Field-Marshal. Invited back to Scotland to command the Covenanters he captured Edinburgh Castle. In 1640 he entered England with the Scots army, routed the King's troops at Newburn, and in 1641, after the Treaty of Ripon, was created Earl of Leven by Charles I to conciliate the Scots. This title is now united with that of Melville. David Leslie, grandson of the 5th Earl, also served in the Swedish army. He later defeated Montrose at Philiphaugh, but was routed by Cromwell at Dunbar in 1650, and imprisoned in the Tower of London for nine years. He became Lord Newark in 1651.

Lindsay

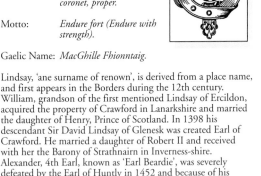

Crest Badge: *A swan rising from a coronet, proper.*

Motto: *Endure fort (Endure with strength).*

Gaelic Name: *MacGhille Fhionntaig.*

Lindsay, 'ane surname of renown', is derived from a place name, and first appears in the Borders during the 12th century. William, grandson of the first mentioned Lindsay of Ercildon, acquired the property of Crawford in Lanarkshire and married the daughter of Henry, Prince of Scotland. In 1398 his descendant Sir David Lindsay of Glenesk was created Earl of Crawford. He married a daughter of Robert II and received with her the Barony of Strathnairn in Inverness-shire. Alexander, 4th Earl, known as 'Earl Beardie', was severely defeated by the Earl of Huntly in 1452 and because of his opposition to James II deprived of all his lands, titles and offices. He was pardoned after a reconciliation. His son David, 5th Earl, was created Duke of Montrose by James III in 1488, the first instance of a dukedom being conferred on a Scotsman not of the Royal family. This dukedom ended with his death in 1495.

John, 1st Earl of Lindsay, assumed the title of Earl of Crawford in 1644. In 1848 the House of Lords decided that the titles of the Earl of Crawford and the Earl of Lindsay belonged to James, 7th Earl of Balcarres, who thus became 24th Earl of Crawford.

Sir David Lindsay of the Mount (1490-1567), poet and reformer, and Robert Lindsay of Pitscottie, author of The Chronicles of Scotland, are two of Scotland's celebrated literary men.

Livingstone

Crest Badge: *A demi- savage wreathed about the head and middle with laurel leaves, in dexter a club, in sinister a serpent entwined round the arm, all proper.*

Motto: *Si je puis (If I can).*

Gaelic Name: *Mac an Léigh (Léigh).*

An ancient name which existed before the 12th century when it appears in charters as Livingston. Sir William Livingston witnessed a charter of the Earl of Lennox in 1270 and from him descended the Livingstons of Livingston. Sir William received the lands of Callendar from David II in 1347. From the Livingstons of Callendar are descended the Livingstones of Westquarter and Kinnaird, of Bonton and of Dunipace.

Sir James Livingston of Callendar was created Lord Livingston in 1458. Alexander, 5th Lord, had charge of the young Queen Mary until after the Battle of Pinkie in 1547. Alexander, 7th Lord, was raised to the earldom of Linlithgow in 1600, but the title was attainted in 1716 because James, 5th Earl, engaged in the Rising of 1715. For the same reason, the viscountcy of Kilsyth, which had been conferred on Sir James Livingstone of Barncloich, was also attained.

The Livingstones of Argyll claim to be descended from a physician to the Lord of the Isles. The Livingstones followed the Stewarts of Appin and accompanied them at the Battle of Culloden where Donald Livingstone saved the banner of the Stewarts. The Livingstone family were Barons of the Bachull and received grants of land in Lismore as keepers of the crozier of the Bishops of Lismore, known in Gaelic as the Bachull Mor. David Livingstone was a descendant of the Argyll family.

Logan

Crest Badge: *A passion nail piercing a human heart, proper.*

Motto: *Hoc majorum virtus (This is the valour of my ancestors).*

Gaelic Name: *Loganaich or Macgill'innein.*

The name Logan appears frequently in the 12th and 13th centuries, and, like the Livingstones, the Logans appear to consist of two distinct families, Lowland and Highland. Lastalrig, or Restalrig, near Edinburgh, was the principal possession of the Logans in the south. Sir Robert, of Restalrig, married a daughter of Robert II, and in 1400 he was appointed Admiral of Scotland. The last Logan of Restalrig was outlawed and died in his residence, Fast Castle, in Berwickshire. Tradition relates that the Logans of the north, Siol Ghillinnein (MacLennans), are descended from the Logans of Drumderfit, in Easter Ross. In the 15th century a feud between the Logans and the Frasers ended in a bloody battle at North Kessock, in which Gilligorm, the chief of the Logans, was killed and his widow carried off by the victors. His widow gave birth to a son who, from his deformity, was known as Crotair MacGilligorm. Educated by the monks at Beauly, on manhood he took Holy Orders at Kilmor in Sleat and in Kilchrinin, Glenelg. Like others of the Highland clergy at that time, he did not remain celibate and his descendants became known as Siol Fhinnein, or MacLennans. At the Battle of Auldearn in 1645, the MacLennans acted as standard bearers to Lord Seaforth, and many were killed. The name MacLennan is still common in Ross-shire.

MacAlister

Crest Badge: *A dexter hand holding a dagger in pale, all proper.*

Motto: *Fortiter (Boldly).*

Gaelic Name: *MacAlasdair.*

This branch of the Clan Donald traces its history back to the 13th century and its origin to Alexander, or Alasdair, son of Donald of Isla and great-grandson of the famous Somerled. The clan territory was principally in Kintyre, and in 1481 Charles Macallestar is designated Steward of Kintyre. Later the clan was numerically strong in Bute and Arran.

The principal family was the MacAlisters of Loup whose chieftain in 1493 was Iain Dubh. This family continued to figure prominently in the history of Kintyre, and their name appears in the General Band of James VI in 1587. Alexander MacAlister of Loup supported James VII and in 1689 fought at Killiecrankie and in 1690 at Cromdale, from which he escaped with some followers to fight again at the Battle of the Boyne. His son Hector died without issue and was succeeded by his brother Charles, who married a daughter of Lamont of Lamont. Charles, 12th of Loup, married Janet Somervill, heiress of Kennox, and asumed the name and arms of Somervill in addition to his own.

An important branch of the clan was the MacAlisters of Tarbert, who were Constables of Tarbert Castle, a stronghold on Loch Fyne built by Robert the Bruce.

Members of the clan who settled in Arran formed a group whose descendants are sometimes referred to as the Clann Allaster Beg.

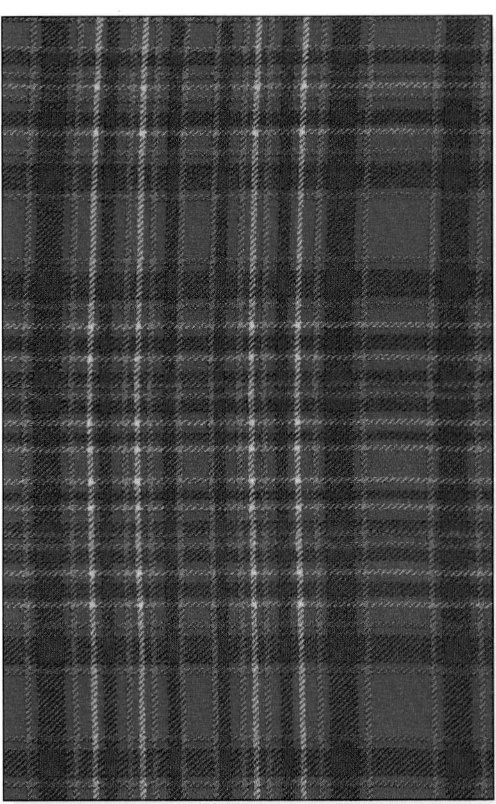

MacArthur

Crest Badge: *Two laurel branches in orle, proper.*

Motto: *Fide et opera (By fidelity and work).*

Gaelic Name: *MacArtuir.*

The Clan MacArthur is of ancient origin. When speaking of olden times, Highlanders in the west would use the proverb, 'There is nothing older, unless, the hills, MacArthur, and the devil'. The clan is claimed to be the older branch of the Clan Campbell, and held the chiefship until the 15th century.

The MacArthurs supported Robert the Bruce in the struggle for the independence of Scotland, and were rewarded with grants of extensive lands in Argyll, including those of the MacDougalls who had opposed the King. The chief was appointed Captain of the Castle of Dunstaffnage. The clan remained powerful until the year 1427 when John, the chief, was executed by order of James I, and thereafter the power of the clan declined.

The MacArthurs of Strachur remained as the principal family of the clan, and it was a member of this family, John MacArthur, born in 1767, who became 'the father of New South Wales'. He accompanied the 102nd Regiment to Sydney in 1790 and was Commandant at Parramatta from 1793 until 1804. He took an interest in the development of the colony, introduced sheep and improved their breed, and in 1817 planted the first vineyard, thus founding the two great Australian industries of wool and wine.

In Skye a family of MacArthurs held land as the hereditary pipers to the MacDonalds of the Isles.

MacAulay

Crest Badge: *An antique boot, couped at the ankle, proper.*

Motto: *Dulce periculum (Danger is sweet).*

Gaelic Name: *MacAmhlaidh.*

Two clans of this name, which means 'son of Olaf', are associated with districts as far apart as Dumbarton and Lewis, but they have no family connection with each other.

Aulay, brother of the Earl of Lennox, signed the Ragman Rolls in 1296, as doing homage to Edward I, but it is as 'of Ardincaple' that we consider them first as a clan. They were a branch of the great Clan Alpine, and in 1591 the chief of the MacAulays entered into a bond of manrent with MacGregor of Glenstrae, admitting to being a cadet of the MacGregors and agreeing to pay the 'calp', a tax due to the chief. 'Awlay Macawlay of Ardincapill' appears in The General Band of 1587 as a vassal of the Duke of Lennox, and again the 'McCawlis' appear in the Roll of Broken Clans in 1594. The MacAulays retained the lands of Ardencaple until the 12th chief sold them to the Duke of Argyll in 1767.

The MacAulays of Lewis were followers of the MacLeods of Lewis, and claim to be descended from Aula, or Olave the Black, who was King of Man and the Isles in the 13th century. The MacAulays of Sutherland and Ross, where they were numerous, were probably related to the Lewis MacAulays. The Ross-shire MacAulays occupied the district round Ullapool and enlisted under the banner of the MacKenzies. Thomas Babington, Lord MacAulay (1800-59), the famous essayist and historian, was descended from the Lewis branch of the clan.

MacBain or MacBean

Crest Badge: *A grey demi cata-mountain, salient, on his sinister foreleg a Highland targe, gules.*

Motto: *Touch not the catt bot a targe.*

Gaelic Name: *MacBheathain.*

The Clan MacBean is of ancient origin and is claimed, by some authorities, to have sprung from the ancient House of Moray. Variations of the name are MacBean, MacBain, and McVean. Originally the MacBeans are said to have come from Lochaber and settled in eastern Inverness-shire. Myles MacBean was a strong supporter of Mackintosh against the Red Comyn, and at the Battle of Harlaw in 1411 many MacBeans fell fighting for Mackintosh. The principal family was the MacBeans of Kinchyle, and Kinchyle signs several important Clan Chattan agreements in 1609, 1664 and 1756. Other families were the MacBeans of Drummond in the parish of Dores, MacBean of Faillie in Strathnairn, and MacBean of Tomatin in Strathdearn. The MacBeans were ever a warlike clan, and at the Battle of Culloden Gillies MacBean, filling a breach in a wall, killed fourteen of the Hanoverian side before he fell. His feat was almost emulated over a century later by Major-General William MacBean, who enlisted in the 93rd Regiment as a private and rose to command it in 1873. He gained the VC for attacking and killing single-handed eleven of the enemy in the main breach of the Begum Bagh at Lucknow in 1858. Another member of the clan, Major Forbes MacBean of the Gordon Highlanders, gained the DSO for his gallant conduct at the taking of the heights of Dargai in 1897.

MacCallum

Crest Badge: *A castle, argent, masoned sable.*

Motto: *In ardua petit (He has attempted difficult things).*

Gaelic Name: *MacChauluim.*

The name MacCallum derives from the Gaelic Mac Ghille Chauluim, 'the son of the servant of Calum', with 'Calum' coming from Colm, the Gaelic form of the Latin Columba, 'dove', and the MacCallum country is in the district of Lorne. The history of the clan is so inextricably connected with that of the Malcolms that it is difficult to separate them. In fact, the two names may correctly be considered as applying to the one clan. The Clan Calum is said to have been originally designated as being of Ariskeodinsh.

Lands in Craignish and on the banks of Loch Avich were granted by Sir Duncan Campbell of Lochow in 1414 to Reginald MacCallum of Corbarron, with the office of hereditary constable of the castles of Lochaffy and Craignish. Corbarron was bequeathed by the last of the family to Zachary MacCallum of Poltalloch in the 17th century. An earlier Zachary of Poltalloch, a supporter of the Marquess of Argyll and renowned for his strength, was killed by Sir Alexander MacDonald at Ederline in 1647. He had slain seven of the enemy when he was attacked by Sir Alexander, and was likely to overpower him also when MacCallum was attacked from behind by a man of the opposing force armed with a scythe. Dugald MacCallum of Poltalloch, who succeeded to the estate in 1779, is said to have been the first to adopt the name Malcolm permanently.

MacDonald

Crest Badge: *Out of coronet a hand in armour fessways, holding by its point a cross crosslet fitchy, gules.*

Motto: *Per mare per terras*
(By sea and by land).

Gaelic Name: *MacDhòmhnuill.*

The most powerful of all the Highland clans, the Clan Donald takes its name from Donald, grandson of Somerled, King of the Isles. The clan held extensive territory, and during Robert the Bruce's struggle to gain Scotland, Alexander, chief of the clan, opposed him. Angus Og, his brother, however, was a strong supporter of Bruce and with a large number of the clan fought for him at Bannockburn. When Bruce succeeded to the throne, Alexander's possessions were granted to Angus. On the death of Bruce, the Clan Donald withdrew their support until they were reconciled to his successor, David II.

Later in the 14th century, John, 1st Lord of the Isles and chief of the clan, divorced his wife Amy and married Margaret, daughter of Robert, High Steward of Scotland, afterwards Robert II. The marriage was indirectly the cause of the Battle of Harlaw in 1411. In 1429 Alexander, 3rd Lord of the Isles, became Earl of Ross, and in revenge for his previous imprisonment he attacked the Crown lands at Inverness and burned the town. James I imposed a crushing defeat on Alexander and he was again imprisoned. The earldom of Ross was annexed to the Crown, and the Lordship of the Isles was forfeited in 1493. Succession passed to the House of Sleat and subsequently a member of this family was created a Baronet of Nova Scotia. In 1776 Sir Alexander MacDonald was created Lord MacDonald.

MacDonald of Sleat

Crest Badge: *A hand in armour in fess, proper, holding by the point a cross crosslet fitchy, gules.*

Motto: *Per mare per terras (By sea and by land).*

Gaelic Name: *MacDhòmhnuill.*

The MacDonalds of Sleat are descended from Hugh, son of Alexander, 3rd Lord of the Isles. He died in 1498 and was succeeded by his son John who died in 1502.

Donald Gruamach, 4th of Sleat, was one of nine island chiefs who submitted to James V in 1538. Donald Gorm, 5th of Sleat, claimed the Lordship of the Isles and the earldom of Ross, but was killed when attempting to capture Eilean Donan Castle in 1539. Donald Gorm Mor, 7th of Sleat, raided the MacLean lands in Mull, but, after being defeated twice, was taken prisoner by the MacLeans. He was released by order of the government which was now taking stronger measures to secure peace in the Western Highlands. Donald and other chiefs were imprisoned in Edinburgh, were heavily fined, and then released. In 1610 Donald and five other chiefs attended Edinburgh, agreed to keep the peace and to submit all disputes to the ordinary courts of law. Donald died without issue in 1616 and was succeeded by his nephew, Sir Donald, 8th of Sleat and 1st Baronet of Sleat. He was created a Baronet of Nova Scotia in 1625 by Charles I for contributing to the establishment of that colony. Sir James, 2nd Baronet, joined Montrose, and in 1651 sent a force to assist Charles II in England. Sir Donald, 4th Baronet, known as 'Donald of the Wars', lost his estates for his part in the Rising of 1715.

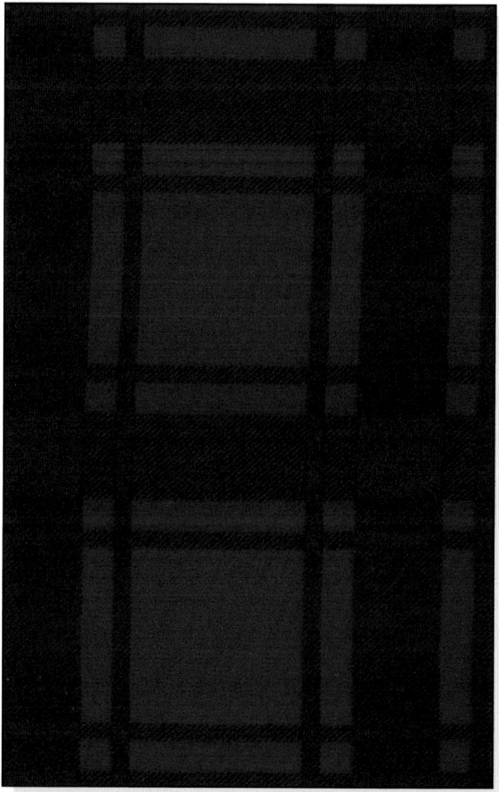

MacDonald of Clanranald

Crest Badge: *On a castle triple towered, an arm in armour, embowed, holding a sword, proper.*

Motto: *My hope is constant in thee.*

Gaelic Name: *MacDhòmhnuill.*

The MacDonalds of Clanranald take their name from Ranald, younger son of John, 1st Lord of the Isles. In 1373 he received a grant of the North Isles and other lands, and from him are descended the families of Moidart, Morar, Knoidart and Glengarry. During the 15th century there were fierce feuds among the branches of Clan Donald, and early in the 16th century Clanranald received from John of Sleat all the latter's estates. On the death of Ranald Bane, 5th chief, the clan, opposing his son Ranald's claim, elected his cousin John of Moidart as chief. In the ensuing struggle, Fraser of Lovat supported Ranald, and John of Moidart was assisted by the MacDonells of Keppoch and the Clan Cameron. At the Battle of Blar-na-Leine in 1544, the Frasers were defeated and John of Moidart kept the chiefship and possessions of Clan Ranald. The MacDonalds of Clanranald served under the Marquess of Montrose in the 17th century. The clan was represented at Killiecrankie by 500 men under the young chief, a boy of sixteen years of age. At Sheriffmuir, the chief of Clanranald was killed, and in 1745 Clanranald was very closely involved with the Rising. It was on Clanranald land that Prince Charles raised his standard, Clanranald supported him throughout his campaign, and it was in Clanranald territory in Benbecula and Uist that the Prince took refuge before embarking for France.

MacDonell of Glengarry

Crest Badge: *A raven, proper, perched on a rock, azure.*

Motto: *Creag an Fhitich (The raven's rock).*

Gaelic Name: *MacDhòmhnuill.*

Ranald, younger son of the 1st Lord of the Isles, was the progenitor of Clanranald, and from his son Donald are descended the MacDonells of Glengarry. Donald and his brothers had been dispossessed of their lands by their uncle, Godfrey, and on the execution of Godfrey's son Alexander in 1427, the lands of Glengarry reverted to the Crown and thereafter the MacDonells became Crown tenants. From Alastair, 4th of Glengarry, the family take their Gaelic patronymic of Mac'ic Alasdair.

Eneas, 9th of Glengarry, was amongst the first to join Montrose and the Royalist army in 1644, and gave devoted service to Montrose and Charles II. He was forfeited by Cromwell in 1651, but at the Restoration in 1660, he was created Lord MacDonell and Aros. The title became extinct on the death of Glengarry in 1680 without male issue. The estates passed to Ranald MacDonell of Scotus.

Alexander, 11th of Glengarry, distinguished himself at Killiecrankie in 1689, where he bore the Royal Standard of James VII, and in 1715 at Sheriffmuir. In the Rising of 1745, 600 Glengarry MacDonells joined Prince Charles under the chief's second son, Angus. Glengarry and his son were imprisoned in the Tower of London. Except for his ruined castle, the estates were sold by the 16th chief whose sons emigrated to New Zealand.

MacDonell of Keppoch

Crest Badge: *A dexter hand holding a cross crosslet, fitchy sable.*

Motto: *Per mare per terras*
(By sea and by land).

Gaelic Name: *MacDhòmhnuill.*

The MacDonells of Keppoch and Garrogach are descended from Alastair Carrach, third son of John, 1st Lord of the Isles, and thus a grandson of Robert II. In 1431 Alastair was forfeited for his part in the insurrection of Donald Balloch, and part of his lands were granted to Mackintosh, chief of Clan Chattan. This caused a long feud between the two clans, and John, 4th of Keppoch, was deposed by the clan for delivering a clansman to the Mackintosh. He was succeeded by his cousin, Donald Glas, whose son Ranald assisted John of Moidart at the 'Battle of the Shirts' in 1544.

Ranald, 9th of Keppoch, an outlaw for most of his life, served in the Swedish army, while Donald Glas, 11th chief, served in the Spanish army. Alexander, 12th of Keppoch, and his brother were murdered in 1663, an event commemorated in Tobair-nan-cean, the 'well of the heads', near Invergarry, where the heads of the seven murderers were washed before being placed before Lord MacDonell of Invergarry. Coll, 15th of Keppoch, known as 'Coll of the Cows', withstood all attempts of the Mackintoshes, assisted by government troops, to capture him, and for forty years he held his lands in Lochaber by right of the sword. He was succeeded by his son Alexander who, with his followers, joined Prince Charles Edward and were the first to strike a blow in the 1745 Rising. Keppoch died fighting single-handed at Culloden.

MacDougall

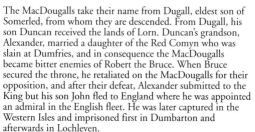

Crest Badge: *On a cup of maintenance a dexter arm in armour embowed, fessways, couped, proper, holding a cross crosslet fitchy, gules.*

Motto: *Buaidh no bàs (To conquer or die).*

Gaelic Name: *MacDhùghaill.*

The MacDougalls take their name from Dugall, eldest son of Somerled, from whom they are descended. From Dugall, his son Duncan received the lands of Lorn. Duncan's grandson, Alexander, married a daughter of the Red Comyn who was slain at Dumfries, and in consequence the MacDougalls became bitter enemies of Robert the Bruce. When Bruce secured the throne, he retaliated on the MacDougalls for their opposition, and after their defeat, Alexander submitted to the King but his son John fled to England where he was appointed an admiral in the English fleet. He was later captured in the Western Isles and imprisoned first in Dumbarton and afterwards in Lochleven.

On the death of King Robert, John of Lorn was released and his lands restored. He married a granddaughter of Robert the Bruce, and his son John was the last MacDougall of Lorn. He died without male issue, and the lands passed, through his daughters, to the Stewarts, Lords of Lorn, in 1388.

In 1457, John Stewart, Lord of Lorn, granted to John MacAlan MacDougall the lands of Dunollie. The clan joined in the Rising of 1715, and were present at Sheriffmuir. On the failure of the Rising, the chief's lands were forfeited but restored when the clan remained loyal to the Crown in 1745.

The eldest daughter of the chief bears the title 'Maid of Lorn'.

MacDuff

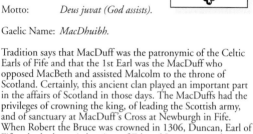

Crest Badge: *A demi-lion rampant, gules, holding in the dexter paw a dagger, proper, hilted and pommelled or.*

Motto: *Deus juvat (God assists).*

Gaelic Name: *MacDhuibh.*

Tradition says that MacDuff was the patronymic of the Celtic Earls of Fife and that the 1st Earl was the MacDuff who opposed MacBeth and assisted Malcolm to the throne of Scotland. Certainly, this ancient clan played an important part in the affairs of Scotland in those days. The MacDuffs had the privileges of crowning the king, of leading the Scottish army, and of sanctuary at MacDuff's Cross at Newburgh in Fife. When Robert the Bruce was crowned in 1306, Duncan, Earl of Fife, who had married a niece of Edward I, was opposed to Bruce, and his sister Isabel, Countess of Buchan and wife of Comyn, Bruce's enemy, was imprisoned in Berwick for seven years.

The old earldom of Fife became extinct in 1353 on the death of Duncan, 12th Earl, but during the succeeding centuries traces of prominent families of the names Duff and MacDuff are found. In 1759 William Duff, Lord Braco, was created Viscount MacDuff and Earl of Fife in the Peerage of Ireland, and in 1827 James, 4th Earl, was raised to the peerage of Great Britain as Baron Fife.

Alexander W.G. Duff, Duke of Fife and Earl of MacDuff, born in 1849, was a successful financier and a founder of the Chartered Company of South Africa. He married Princess Louise, daughter of Edward VII, in 1889. He died in 1912 and was succeeded by his daughter, Princess Alexandra Victoria, who married Prince Arthur of Connaught.

MacEwen

Crest Badge: *The trunk of an oak tree from which sprouts forth young branches, proper.*

Motto: *Reviresco (I grow strong).*

Gaelic Name: *MacEòghainn.*

Although of ancient origin, there are few authentic records of this clan. A genealogy in a 15th-century manuscript proved that the Clan MacEwen existed long before 1450 and that they were known as the MacEwens of Otter. The Reverend Alexander McFarlane, minister of the parish of Kilfinan, writing in 1794, states that 'On a rocky point on the coast of Lochfyne about a mile below the church of Kilfinan is to be seen the vestige of a building called Caisteal mhic Eoghuin or MacEwen's Castle. This MacEwen was the chief of a clan and proprietor of Otter.'

Eoghain na h-Oitrich, 'Ewen of Otter', who gives his name to the clan, lived at the beginning of the 13th century. Gillespie, 5th of Otter, flourished about a century later. Swene MacEwen, 9th and last of Otter, granted lands of Otter to Duncan Campbell in 1432 and resigned the barony of Otter to James I, but it was returned to him with remainder to Celestine, son and heir of Duncan Campbell of Lochow. In 1513 James V confirmed the barony of Otter to Colin, Earl of Argyll, and thereafter Otter remained in the possession of the Campbells. Without lands the MacEwens became a 'broken' clan and found their way to many districts. A large number settled in the Lennox country, others went farther afield, to Lochaber, Perth, Skye, and the Lowlands, including Galloway.

MacFarlane

Crest Badge: *A demi-savage holding in dexter hand a sword and in sinister an imperial crown, all proper.*

Motto: *This I'll defend.*

Gaelic Name: *MacPhàrlain.*

The Loch Lomond district was the home of several war-like clans, including the MacFarlanes who trace their descent from Gilchrist, brother of Maldowen, 3rd of the ancient Earls of Lennox in the 13th century. The great-grandson of Gilchrist was named Bartholomew, and from its Gaelic equivalent, Parlan, the clan takes its name.

Duncan, 6th chief, obtained the lands of Arrochar from the Earl of Lennox and, by marriage in 1395, acquired many of the adjoining lands. On the death without male issue of the last of the old Earls of Lennox, MacFarlane claimed the title and lands. The conferring of the earldom on Sir John Stewart of Darnley led to an enmity between the families that ended only when a MacFarlane cadet married a daughter of the Earl of Lennox in the 15th century.

In 1493 the son of this line assumed the title of Captain of the Clan MacFarlane, and thereafter the clan supported the Earls of Lennox. Their war-like spirit took them to Flodden in 1513, Pinkie in 1547 and Langside in 1568, where they fought against Queen Mary and captured three of her standards.

In the 16th and 17th centuries the clan was proscribed and deprived of lands and name. Some members of the clan emigrated to Ireland, and the last chief is believed to have emigrated to America in the 18th century.

Walter, 20th chief, who died in 1767, was a famous antiquarian and genealogist of his time.

Macfie

Crest Badge: *A demi-lion rampant, proper.*

Motto: *Pro rege (For the king).*

Gaelic Name: *MacDubh-shithe.*

The island of Colonsay is the ancient home of the Macduffies or Macphees, a branch of the great Clan Alpine, said to be descended from Kenneth MacAlpine, King of Scots. The early history of the clan is unknown, but Donald Macduffie witnessed a charter at Dingwall in 1463, and Macfie of Colonsay was one of the principal chiefs who met Bishop Knox of the Isles and signed the Bond and Statues of Iona in 1609, an attempt to impose order and peace in the area. In 1615 Malcolm Macfie of Colonsay joined in the rebellion of Sir James MacDonald. He was later delivered to the Earl of Argyll by Coll Kitto MacDonald who, in 1623, was charged with his murder. Colonsay passed to the MacDonalds and then to the MacNeils.

When the Macfies were dispossessed, some of them followed the MacDonalds and others settled in the Cameron country of Lochaber and supported that clan at the Battle of Culloden. In Galloway the name took the form of Macguffie and Machaffie. Ewen Macphee who lived in the middle of the 19th century was famous as the last of the Scottish 'outlaws'. He enlisted in the army but deserted as a result of a misunderstanding and settled with his family on an island on Loch Quoich. He recognised no law and no landowner, resided rent free and defended his home with firearms, his wife being as proficient in their use as he. He held it until, in his old age, he was ejected for sheep stealing.

MacGillivray

Crest Badge: *A stag's head couped,
proper, tyned or.*

Motto: *Dunmaglas.*

Gaelic Name: *MacGhille-brath.*

This clan, one of the oldest branches of the Clan Chattan
confederation, came originally from Morven and Lochaber,
where they were one of the principal clans in the time of
Somerled, recognized by the Norse as King of the Isles. They
suffered severely, as did many others, during the conquest by
Alexander II in the 13th century. This may have been why,
according to a 16th-century historian, Gillivray, the progenitor
of the clan, vicGillivray, whose name means 'son of the lover of
knowledge', chose to take protection from the Farquhard
Mackintosh, 5th of Mackintosh.

About 1500 the MacGillivrays settled at Dunmaglass in
Strathnairn, and in succeeding years added considerably to
their possessions. They became influential in that part of the
country and took a prominent part in public affairs and local
clan disputes. The Clan Chattan Bonds of 1609 and 1664 were
signed by three members of the clan.

The MacGillivrays were active in the Risings of 1715 and
1745, losing their chief and many others at Culloden. The
chief's brother William survived the battle and, assisted by
another brother, was able to increase the family estate. On the
death of William's son there followed lawsuits over the
succession which eventually in 1858 passed to the Dalcrombie
line. They soon sold Dunmaglass, to leave the clan landless in
its own country by 1890.

MacGregor

Crest Badge: *A lion's head, erased, crowned with an antique crown, proper.*

Motto: *'S rioghal mo dhream (Royal is my race).*

Gaelic Name: *MacGrioghair.*

'S rioghal mo dhream, 'Royal is my race', is the claim of this, one of the most famous of Highland clans, and the principal branch of the Clan Alpine. The clan claims descent from Griogar, son of Alpin, King of Dalriada in the 8th century. The home of the clan was on the border of Argyll and Perthshire and included Glenorchy, Glenstrae, Glenlyon and Glengyle. The earliest lands of the clan, Glenorchy, previously owned by the Campbells, was bestowed on the MacGregors for services rendered to Alexander II in his conquest of Argyll. For a long time the MacGregors kept possession of their lands by right of the sword, but the enmity of surrounding clans resulted in attempts to displace them, and their inevitable retaliation earned them the reputation of being a turbulent clan. During these conflicts the Campbells were able to obtain grants of MacGregor lands, the name of MacGregor was proscribed, and severe enactments were passed against the clan whose members were prosecuted and persecuted. Charles II, because of their support, repealed the acts against Clan Gregor, but upon the accession of William of Orange the acts of proscription were renewed, and it was not until 1775 that the penal statutes against the MacGregors were finally repealed. Rob Roy (1671-1734), the celebrated freebooter and hero of Sir Walter Scott's romance, was a son of Colonel Donald MacGregor of Glengyle.

MacInnes

Crest Badge: *An arm in band from the*
shoulder, hand proper, and
attired in a highland coatee
of the proper tartan of the
Clann Aonghais, grasping
a bow sable, stringed or.

Motto: *Irìd Ghibht Dhè Agus An Righ*
(Through the grace of God and the King).

Gaelic Name: *MacAonghais.*

The MacInneses, or Clann Aonghais, are a Celtic clan of
ancient origin. The earliest known territory of the MacInneses
was Morven, and they are said to have formed part of a branch
of the Siol Gillebride, believed to be the original inhabitants of
Morven and Ardnamurchan. It is claimed that they were
constables of the castle of Kinlochaline.

Hugh MacDonald, the Sleat historian of the 17th century,
writing of Morven in the 12th century, states that 'the principal
names in the country were MacInnes and MacGillivray, who
are the same as the MacInnes', and then goes on to describe
how Somerled, coming out of his retirement to do so, led these
clans and defeated the Norsemen and expelled them from the
district. The MacInneses remained in possession of Morven, and
as late as 1645 it appears that a MacInnes was in command
of the castle of Kinlochaline when it was besieged and burnt by
Coll Kitto MacDonald.

When the MacInneses and the MacGillivrays of Morven and
Ardgour were broken up, they acknowledged the Clan Dugall
Craignish (Campbell) as their chief.

The hereditary bowmen to the chiefs of MacKinnon were a
branch of the MacInneses, and this may be the origin of the
MacInneses in Skye.

Macintyre

Crest Badge: *A dexter hand holding a skean 'dhu in pale, on which is affixed a snow ball all proper. Around the wrist a manche of the correct tartan turned or.*

Motto: *Per ardua (Through difficulties).*

Gaelic Name: *Mac an t-Saoir.*

The commonly accepted origin of the name is that Mac an t-Saoir means 'the son of the carpenter'. However, a prominent member of the clan gives the derivation as from a MacDonald, called Cean-tires because he possessed lands in Kintyre. His son John acquired the lands of Deguish in Lorn and was known as John Mac-Cein-teire-Dheguish.

A branch of the Macintyres was a sept of the Campbells of Craignish. The principal family of the clan proper were the Macintyres who held the lands of Glenoe on Loch Etive for several centuries until they were forced to part with them in 1806. Members of this family emigrated to America.

The clan was notable for its versatility. The Macintyres of Glenoe were hereditary foresters to the Stewarts, Lords of Lorn. The Macintyres of Badenoch are descended from the bard Macintyre whom William, 13th of Mackintosh, took under his protection in 1496. A family of Macintyres were hereditary pipers to MacDonald of Clanranald, and the Macintyres of Rannoch were hereditary pipers to the chief of Clan Menzies. A famous Gaelic poet was Duncan Macintyre, Donnachadh Ban Mac an t-Saoir, born in Glenorchy in 1724. He was in government service during the Rising of 1745 but was later imprisoned for a poem he wrote against the Act proscribing Highland dress.

MacIver

Crest Badge: *A boar's head, couped, or.*

Motto: *Nunquam obliviscar*
(I will never forget).

Gaelic Name: *Mac Iomhair.*

The Clan Iver are claimed to have been part of the army of Alexander II which conquered Argyll in 1221, for which they received lands in that district. They had come from Glenlyon, and in Argyll their principal lands were Lergachonzie and Asknish, and in Glassary and Cowal.

The clan's history after obtaining their Argyll lands is obscure. In the 13th century branches of the clan left Argyll to settle in Lochaber, Glenelg and Ross, and it would appear that the MacIvers were for some time a 'broken' clan, without land. In 1564 Archibald, 5th Earl of Argyll, renounced all claims to the 'calps', or gifts due to the chief, of any of the Clan Iver. Duncan, who succeeded as chief of the clan about 1572, is described as of Stronshiray and Superior of Lergachonzie. In 1685 Iver of Asknish and Stronshiray forfeited land for aiding Archibald, 9th Earl of Argyll, in rebellion against James VII. Following the Glorious Revolution of 1688, Archibald, 10th Earl, restored the estates of Iver to his son Duncan MacIver on condition that he and his heirs should bear the name and arms of Campbell. Iver was thus the last chief of the MacIvers, and Sir Humphrey Campbell who died in 1818 was the last in the male line of Duncan MacIver of Stronshiray.

Branches of the clan in the north and in Lewis retained the name of MacIver.

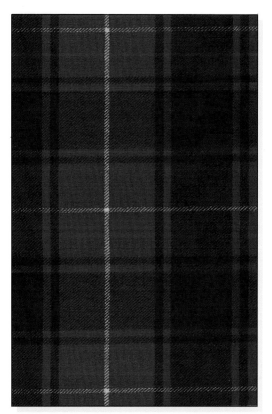

MacKay

Crest Badge: *A dexter cubit arm, holding erect a dagger in pale, all proper, hilt and pommel or. (The badge shown is that of the Chief and worn by him alone. Clansmen wear the crest badge without coronet and feathers).*

Motto: *Manu forti (With a strong hand).*

Gaelic Name: *MacAoidh.*

This powerful clan was known as the Clan Morgan and as the Clann Aoidh. The former name is claimed from Morgan, son of Magnus, in the early 14th century, the latter from his grandson Aoidh, or Hugh. The MacKays are descended from the old Royal house of MacEth.

When Donald, 2nd Lord of the Isles, invaded Sutherland in pursuit of his claim to the earldom of Ross, he was opposed by Angus Dubh and the Clan MacKay, who were defeated and Angus imprisoned by the Lord of the Isles. Angus, however, became reconciled and married Elizabeth, daughter of his captor, with whom he received many lands. Angus was killed at the time of the Battle of Drumnacoub in 1429.

In 1626 Sir Donald MacKay of Farr raised an army of 3,000 men for service in Bohemia and afterwards in Denmark, and was created Lord Reay. The lands of Strathnaver were sold in 1642, and the remainder of the MacKay country was sold in 1829 to the house of Sutherland. Aeneas, grandson of the 1st Lord Reay, was colonel of the MacKay Dutch regiment and settled in Holland where his family were ennobled as Barons, and when the Scottish succession ceased, Baron Eric MacKay van Ophement, Holland, became 12th Baron Reay.

MacKenzie

Crest Badge: *A mountain inflamed, proper. (MacKenzie more commonly use the badge a stag's head cabossed or, and the motto 'Cuidich 'n righ'- Help the king).*

Motto: *Luceo non uro (I shine, not burn).*

Gaelic Name: *MacCoinnich.*

The MacKenzies claim to be descended from Colin, progenitor of the Earls of Ross. He died in 1278 and was succeeded by his son Kenneth. In 1362 Murdoch, son of Kenneth, 3rd Earl, received from David II the lands of Kintail.

In 1466 the MacKenzies defeated the MacDonalds in battle at Blair-na-park. The clan supported James IV at Flodden in 1513, where their chief was captured by the English, and at the Battle of Pinkie in 1547 they fought for James V. Colin, 11th chief, fought in the army of Queen Mary at Langside in 1568. Kenneth, 12th chief, in 1607 received a charter of the lands of Lochalsh and Lochcarron, and it is said that at this time all the lands from Ardnamurchan to Strathnaver were in the possession of the MacKenzies or their vassals. Kenneth was created MacKenzie of Kintail in 1609.

Colin, 2nd Lord was created Earl of Seaforth by James VI in 1623, and was Secretary of State in Scotland to Charles II. Kenneth, 4th Earl, was nominated a Knight of the Thistle by James VII whom he followed to France. William, 5th Earl, joined the Earl of Mar in 1715, was at Sherrifmuir and later escaped to France. He was attainted and his estates forfeited. In 1726, he was pardoned by George I and died in Lewis in 1740. Kenneth, his grandson, repurchased the forfeited estates and in 1771 was restored to the earldom of Seaforth

MacKinnon

Crest Badge: *A boar's head erased,*
argent, in mouth a deer's
shankbone, proper.

Motto: *Audentes fortuna juvat*
(Fortune assists the daring).

Gaelic Name: *MacFhionghuin.*

The MacKinnons, one of the branches of the Siol Alpine, claim
to be descended from Fingon, a great-grandson of Kenneth
MacAlpin.

The MacKinnons held lands in Mull and Skye, and appear to
have been vassals of the Lords of the Isles. In 1409, Lachlan
MacKinnon witnessed a charter of Donald, 2nd MacDonald
Lord of the Isles. Until the forfeiture of the Lordship, the
history of the MacKinnons is bound up with that important
family. The MacKinnons were also closely connected with the
ecclesiastical history of Iona, whose last abbot was John
MacKinnon, who died in 1550.

In 1542, Ewen, chief of the clan, received from James V the
lands of Mishnish and Strathardle. The clan was at the Battle
of Inverlochy under Montrose in 1645. In 1646, the chief,
Lauchlan, and the clan supported Charles II at the Battle of
Worcester. Lauchlan's second son, Donald, emigrated to
Antigua, where he died in 1720.

The MacKinnons were out in the Rising of 1715 and again in
1745 in support of the Stuarts. After Culloden, the chief, old
and infirm, was imprisoned in London but was allowed to
return home in 1747. His son Charles had to part with the
family estates after they had been in the clan's possession for
over four centuries. In 1808, the last chief of the main line
died, and the chiefship passed to the family of Donald
MacKinnon in Antigua.

Mackintosh

Crest Badge: *A cat salient gardant, proper.*

Motto: *Touch not the cat bot a glove (Touch not the cat without a glove).*

Gaelic Name: *Mac an Toisich.*

The clan name is derived from Mac an Toisich and means 'son of the chief'. The founder of the clan is said to have been a son of MacDuff, ancestor of the Earls of Fife. The Mackintoshes are one of the clans forming the Clan Chattan confederation, the chiefship of which came to the chiefs of Mackintosh through the marriage in 1291 of Angus, 6th Laird of Mackintosh, to Eva, heiress of Clan Chattan.

The first mention of the Mackintosh as Captain of Clan Chattan is in a charter granted to William Mackintosh by the Lord of the Isles in 1337 and confirmed by David II in 1359. In 1639, Mackintosh joined the Covenanters north of the Spey, and he formed part of the army opposing Cromwell in 1650. At the Glorious Revolution, the Mackintoshes supported the new government and refused to join Viscount Dundee.

They were prominent in the Jacobite Rising of 1715 under Brigadier Mackintosh of Borlum. Angus, chief in 1745, was on government service with Loudon's Highlanders when the Rising took place, but Lady Anne, his wife, who was a Farquharson of Invercauld, raised the clan for Prince Charles, and her strategy was responsible for the Rout of Moy in 1746 when 1,500 of the government's troops were put to flight by half a dozen of 'Colonel Anne's' retainers. Following the death in 1938 of the 18th chief, the chiefships of Clan Mackintosh and Clan Chattan were separated.

MacLachlan

Crest Badge: *Out of crest coronet a castle, triple towered, proper.*

Motto: *Fortis et fidus*
(Brave and trusty).

Gaelic Name: *Mac Lachlainn.*

The MacLachlans are of ancient origin. As early as 1230, Gilchrist MacLachlan witnessed a charter granted by Laumun, ancestor of the Lamonds. In 1291, Gilleskel MacLachlan received a charter of his lands in Argyll from John Baliol, and in 1308 Gillespie MacLachlan was a member of the first parliament of Robert the Bruce in St Andrews. During the 14th and 15th centuries, the chiefs of the clan made grants to the Preaching Friars of Glasgow from their lands of Kilbride. The MacLachlans were adherents of the Lordship of the Isles until its forfeiture, when they became independent. A Campbell connection is argued for a branch which provided for some centuries the hereditary captains of the Campbell castle of Innischonnel, the great fortress of Lochow. The MacLachlans of Coire-uanan, in Lochaber, were hereditary standard-bearers to Cameron of Lochiel.

In 1615, the MacLachlans formed part of the Earl of Argyll's army that opposed the forces of Sir James MacDonald of Isla, and in 1689 they were with Dundee at the Battle of Killiecrankie. During the 1745 Rising the clan supported Prince Charles, and the chief, who had been appointed ADC to the Prince, was killed at Culloden. The estates were attainted, but in 1749 Robert, then chief, regained them, and from him are descended the later chiefs.

There are several branches of the clan in Argyll, Perthshire, Stirlingshire and Lochaber.

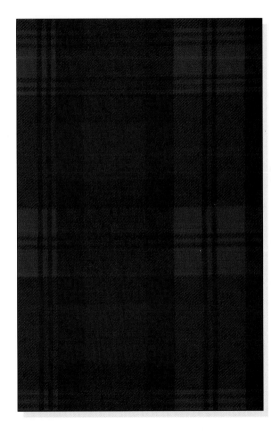

MacLaine of Lochbuie

Crest Badge: *A battleaxe in pale with twobranches in saltire dexter a laurel, sinister a cypress, all proper.*

Motto: *Vincere vel mori (To conquer or die).*

Gaelic Name: *MacGhille Eoin.*

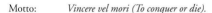

The MacLaines of Lochbuie were descended from Eachan Reaganach, brother of Lachlan, progenitor of the MacLeans of Duart. Eachan, or Hector, received the lands of Lochbuie from John, 1st Lord of the Isles, his brother's father-in-law. Hector's son Charles was the progenitor of the MacLeans of Dochgarroch, a sept of Clan Chattan.

John Og, of Lochbuie, received from James IV charters confirming the lands and baronies held by his progenitor. He was killed with two of his sons in a feud with the MacLeans of Duart, and the surviving son, Murdoch was taken to Ireland for safety. Returning, when he reached manhood, he captured Lochbuie Castle with the aid of his childhood nurse, who had recognized him. In Edinburgh, before king and court, his son John Mor, an expert swordsman, fought and killed a famous Italian fencer who had challenged all Scotland.

The MacLaines were strong supporters of the Stuarts, formed part of the army of Montrose, and afterwards fought at Killiecrankie in 1689 under Viscount Dundee. In later years, they found scope for their military activities in the European and American wars of the 18th century.

Donald, 20th of Lochbuie, born in 1816, amassed a fortune as an East India merchant and saved Lochbuie for the family by clearing its debts. The estate has now passed out of the family.

MacLaren

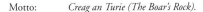

Crest Badge: *A lion's head sabled langued or, crowned with an antique crown or, the four points argent, surrounded by laurel in orle proper.*

Motto: *Creag an Turie (The Boar's Rock).*

Gaelic Name: *MacLabhruinn.*

The MacLarens are traditionally descended from Lorn, son of Erc, who landed in Argyll in AD 503, and are recorded in the 12th century as having lands in Balquhidder and Strathearn. In the Ragman Rolls in 1296, which lists those giving allegiance to Edward I, are three names identified as belonging to the clan - Maurice of Tyrie, Conan of Balquhidder, and Laurin of Ardveche in Strathearn. In the 14th century, when the earldom of Strathearn became vested in the Crown, the MacLarens were reduced from being proprietors of their lands to perpetual tenants. They remained loyal to the Crown, however, and fought for James III at Sauchieburn in 1488, for James IV at Flodden in 1513, and for Mary Queen of Scots at Pinkie in 1547 and appear in the Rolls of the Clans in 1587 and 1594. The MacLarens were a war-like clan and had their share of feuds. The greater part of the clan followed the Stewarts of Appin, others following the Murrays of Atholl. Dugal Stewart, 1st of Appin, was the natural son of John Stewart, Lord of Lorn, and a daughter of MacLaren of Ardveche. The clan was out in the 1745 Rising and suffered severely at Culloden. MacLaren of Invernenty was taken prisoner but made a remarkable escape near Moffat when being taken to Carlisle, an incident described in Sir Walter Scott's *Redgauntlet*.

MacLean

Crest Badge: *A tower embattled, argent.*

Motto: *Virtue mine honour.*

Gaelic Name: *MacGhille Eoin.*

The Clan MacLean are descended from Gilleathain na Tuaidh, Gillean of the Battleaxe, in the 13th century. Two brothers, his descendants, were Lachlan Lubanach, progenitor of the MacLeans of Duart, and Eachan Reaganach, progenitor of the MacLaines of Lochbuie.

The MacLeans were supporters of the MacDougalls of Lorn, but later transferred their allegiance to the MacDonalds, Lords of the Isles, and became one of their most powerful vassals. The MacLeans fought at the Battle of Harlaw in 1411, where their chief was killed. On the forfeiture of the Lordship of the Isles in 1493, the MacLeans became independent.

During the 16th and 17th centuries, the MacLeans were one of the most important clans in the Western Isles. In 1632, Lachlan MacLean of Morven, heir to Hector MacLean of Duart, was created a baronet. MacLeans fought at Inverlochy in 1645 under Montrose and at Inverkeithing in 1651. In the latter battle occurred a famous incident when seven brothers in the clan died to protect their chief, each as he fell shouting, 'Another for Hector'. The sacrifice was unavailing, for Sir Hector too was killed. The MacLeans supported Dundee at the Battle of Killiecrankie in 1689, and joined the Earl of Mar in 1715. Sir Hector, chief in 1745, was imprisoned in London for two years, but the clan appeared at Culloden under the Duke of Perth.

MacLeod

Crest Badge: *A bull's head, cabossed sable, horned or, between two flags, gules, staves sable.*

Motto: *Hold fast.*

Gaelic Name: *MacLeòid.*

The Clan MacLeod is descended from Leod, son of Olave the Black, King of the Isles, who lived in the 13th century. Leod's two sons, Tormod and Torquil, were founders of the two main branches of the clan. From Tormod came the MacLeods of Glenelg, Harris and Dunvegan, and from Torquil the MacLeods of Lewis, Waternish and Assynt, which were dispossessed in the 16th century.

The Siol Tormod supported Bruce in the War of Independence, and about 1343 Malcolm, son of Tormod, received a charter from David II, granting him lands in Glenelg. John, 6th of Glenelg, supported the Lord of the Isles at Harlaw in 1411. In 1498, James IV granted to Alexander, 8th of Glenelg, the lands of Duirnish and Troternish, and in the charter his father, William, 7th of Glenelg, was described as of Dunvegan.

A distinguished chief was Roderick, 16th of Dunvegan, known as Rory Mor, who in 1595 took a group of men to Ulster to take part in O'Neill's revolt. Knighted by James VI in 1603, he was held in high esteem by the clan, and his death in 1626 was the subject of the piobaireachd, Rory Mor's Lament, composed by Patrick Mor MacCrimmon.

The MacLeods supported Charles I and Charles II and were present at the Battle of Worcester in 1651, when the clan was almost wiped out. This may account for the MacLeods not taking part in the later Jacobite Risings.

Macmillan

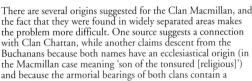

Crest Badge: *A dexter and a sinister hand brandishing a two-handed sword, proper.*

Motto: *Miseris succurrere disco (I learn to succour the distressed).*

Gaelic Name: *MacGhille-Mhaolain.*

There are several origins suggested for the Clan Macmillan, and the fact that they were found in widely separated areas makes the problem more difficult. One source suggests a connection with Clan Chattan, while another claims descent from the Buchanans because both names have an ecclesiastical origin (in the Macmillan case meaning 'son of the tonsured [religious]') and because the armorial bearings of both clans contain a rampant lion.

The Macmillans were in the Loch Arkaig district in the 12th century, when it is alleged they were removed to the Crown lands round Loch Tay. About two centuries later they were driven from Lawers, and the greater number settled in Knapdale, while the others travelled farther south. The branch in Galloway is claimed to be of the latter number.

Macmillan of Knap was considered to be the chief of the clan, and when the Knapdale Macmillans died out, the chiefship passed to the family of Dunmore, an estate on the opposite side of Loch Tarbet, which also died out.

There were Macmillans in Lochaber, who followed Cameron of Lochiel, and others of Urquhart and Glenmoriston who followed Grant of Glenmoriston. An Argyllshire branch is descended from the Lochaber Macmillans.

By decree of Lyon Court, the chiefship passed to the representative of the Laggalgarve line in 1951.

Macnab

Crest Badge: *A savage's head affronté,*
proper.

Motto: *Timor omnis abesto*
(Let fear be far from all).

Gaelic Name: *Mac an Aba.*

The Clan Macnab, a branch of the Siol Alpine, are of
ecclesiastical origin, being termed in Gaelic Clann-an-Aba,
'children of the abbot', and claim descent from the abbots of
Glendochart in Perthshire, where the clan lands were for several
centuries. As early as the 12th century they were an important
clan, but they joined the MacDougalls in their fight against
Robert the Bruce.

After Bannockburn, the Macnabs lost all their lands except the
Barony of Bovain in Glendochart, which was confirmed to
them by a charter from David II to Gilbert Macnab in 1336.
Towards the end of the 15th century, Finlay, 4th chief, added
greatly to the family estates. In 1552, however, Finlay, 6th
chief, mortgaged most of his lands to Campbell of Glenorchy,
but the clan refused to acknowledge Glenorchy's superiority. In
1606, Finlay, 7th chief, entered into a bond of friendship with
his cousin, Lachlan MacKinnon of Strathardle, which is often
quoted as proof of their common descent.

The Macnabs, under their chief 'Smooth John', supported the
Stuarts during the Civil Wars, and the chief was killed at the
Battle of Worcester in 1651. In 1745, the then chief sided with
the government but the clan supported Prince Charles. Francis,
12th and last chief in the direct male line, was a noted eccentric
and the subject, in Highland dress, of Raeburn's striking
portrait.

MacNaughton

Crest Badge: *A castle embattled, gules.*

Motto: *I hope in God.*

Gaelic Name: *MacNeachdainn.*

The progenitor of this ancient clan, whose name means 'son of the pure one', is alleged to be Nachtan Mor, who died in the 10th century. The clan is supposed to be one of those transferred by Malcolm IV from the Province of Moray to the Crown lands in Strathtay in Perthshire in the 12th century. About a century later, they held lands on Loch Awe and Loch Fyne, and in 1267 Alexander III appointed Gilchrist MacNaughton and his heirs keepers of the castle of Fraoch Eilean in Loch Awe. The MacNaughtons also held the castles of Dubh-Loch in Glenshira and Dunderave on Loch Fyne. Donald MacNaughton opposed Bruce and as a result lost most of his possessions, but in the reign of David II the fortunes of the MacNaughtons were somewhat restored by the grant of lands in Lewis. Alexander, chief of the clan, who was knighted by James IV, was killed at the Battle of Flodden in 1513. The MacNaughtons remained loyal to the Stuarts, and after the Restoration, the then chief, Alexander, was knighted by Charles II. His son John fought at Killiecrankie in 1698. The estates passed out of the family about 1691, having been forfeited to the Crown.

The last chief of Dunderave died in Edinburgh in 1773, a retired Inspector-General of Customs, and after a gap of fifty years, the chiefship fell to the MacNaughtens, a branch of the family that had settled in Ireland in the reign of Elizabeth I.

MacNeill

Crest Badge: *A rock.*

Motto: *Vincere vel mori*
(To conquer or die).

Gaelic Name: *MacNèill.*

There were two main branches of the Clan MacNeill, the
MacNeills of Barra and the MacNeills of Gigha. The clan were
vassals of the Lords of the Isles, and in 1427 Gilleonan received
from his overlord a charter of Barra and the lands of Boisdale in
South Uist, which charter was confirmed in 1495 by James IV
after the forfeiture of the lands of the Lords of the Isles.
The MacNeills of Barra subsequently supported the MacLeans
of Duart, while the MacNeills of Gigha followed the
MacDonalds of Isla, and in the feuds between the MacLeans
and the MacDonalds the two branches of the MacNeills were
often fighting on opposing sides.
Of the Barra branch, General Roderick MacNeill, last of the
direct line, had to part with the island, which he sold in 1838.
The chiefship was successfully claimed by Robert L. MacNeill,
who re-acquired parts of the island in 1938 and restored
Kisimul Castle, the MacNeills' 13th century stronghold which
was abandoned in the 18th century.
When Neil, the last chief of the Gigha branch, was killed in
1530, the chiefship passed to the MacNeills of Taynish, and in
1590 Hector of Taynish repurchased Gigha, which had been
sold in 1554. In 1780 Gigha was sold to the MacNeills of
Colonsay, who had obtained Colonsay from the Duke of Argyll
in 1700. Colonsay remained with the MacNeill family until
1904.

MacNicol or Nicolson

Crest Badge: *A hawk's head erased, gules.*

Motto: *Sgorra Bhreac.(Grey ridge)*

Gaelic Name: *MacNeacail.*

In the Statistical Account of Scotland of 1841, the Reverend William MacKenzie writes of Assynt: 'Tradition and even documents declare that it was a forest of the ancient Thanes of Sutherland. One of these Prince Thanes gave it in vassalage to one Mackrycul'. Mackrycul has been identified as Gregall, mentioned in an early genealogy of the MacNicols, but on the marriage of Torquil MacLeod to the daughter of the last of the MacNicol chiefs, Assynt passed to the MacLeods.

The MacNicols seem first to have removed to Skye, where they settled at various places on the island, but Nicolson of Scorrybreac was always regarded as the chief of the clan in the west, and these lands remained in the family for several centuries.

Though its history is meagre, the clan was certainly of some importance on Skye. The Reverend Donald Nicolson, chief of the Scorrybreac family at the end of the 17th century, was minister of Trotternish and resigned in 1696 only because of his opposition to the Presbyterian Church of Scotland.

Alexander Nicolson, who was born at Hugobost in 1827, was a member of the commission appointed in 1883 to enquire into crofting conditions.

There were MacNicols in Glenorchy who were said to be descended from a Nicol Macphee who left Lochaber in the 16th century, and Andrew Nicolson was a Norse baron who distinguished himself at the Battle of Largs in 1263.

Macpherson

Crest Badge: *A cat sejant, proper.*

Motto: *Touch not the cat bot a glove (Touch not the cat without a glove).*

Gaelic Name: *Mac a' Phearsoin, MacMhuirich.*

Macpherson is a name of ecclesiastical origin, meaning 'son of the parson'. The clan formed a branch of the Clan Chattan confederation and disputed its leadership with the Mackintoshes.

There seem to have been several families of Macphersons, but the family of Cluny in Inverness-shire emerged as the most important. One Andrew is recorded in Cluny in 1603, and in 1609 he signed the Clan Chattan Bond, taking on the burden of the Brin and other families of the Macphersons.

In 1640, Donald Macpherson of Cluny was a faithful royalist. In 1715, the Macphersons were active under their chief, Duncan, on the Stuart side, and during the Rising of 1745, Ewen Macpherson of Cluny with 600 of the clan, joined Prince Charles and acted with great gallantry at several engagements, but did not arrive in time to take part in the Battle of Culloden. Cluny himself, however, actively assisted Prince Charles to escape capture. Consequently, the house of Cluny was burned to the ground and for nine years the chief remained in hiding, mainly on his own estate, in a shelter of trees and brushwood constructed on the side of Ben Alder. In spite of a reward of £1,000 he was never captured and ultimately escaped to France in 1755. The Cluny estates were, of course, forfeited, but in 1784 they were restored to Ewen's son, Duncan. Cluny Castle was rebuilt and remained the home of the chief until 1932.

Macquarrie

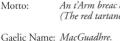

Crest Badge: *Out of an antique crown a bent arm in armour holding a dagger.*

Motto: *An t'Arm breac dearg. (The red tartaned army).*

Gaelic Name: *MacGuadhre.*

The Macquarries are one of the branches of the great Clan Alpine, and when Alexander II invaded the Western Highlands in 1249 he was joined by Cormac Mor, chief of the Macquarries, but it is not until the death of John Macquarrie of Ulva in 1473 that there is any authentic record of the clan. Twenty years later, John's son, Dunslaff, was chief and the clan lands were the island of Ulva and part of Mull. After the forfeiture of the Lordship of the Isles, the clan acquired independence and then followed the MacLeans of Duart, although supporting Donald Dubh MacDonald in his effort to restore the Lordship of the Isles in 1503. In 1505, the Macquarries, with their leaders, the MacLeans of Duart, submitted to the government, and in 1517 Dunslaff Macquarrie was included in the petition of Lachlan MacLean of Duart for a free remission for all offences, which was granted by the Privy Council.

The Macquarries never recovered from the blow suffered in 1651 when the chief, Allan Macquarrie, and most of the clan were killed at the Battle of Inverkeithing by Cromwell's troops. Lachlan, 16th of Ulva, who had entertained Dr Johnson and Boswell in 1773, was forced to sell his lands in 1778. He died in 1818, aged 103, and was the last-known chief.

Major-General Lachlan Macquarrie was Governor of New South Wales in Australia from 1809 to 1821 and is commemorated in Macquarrie Island.

Macqueen

Crest Badge: *A wolf rampant ermine holding a pheon gules point downward argent.*

Motto: *Constant and faithful.*

Gaelic Name: *MacShuibhne.*

The Clan Macqueen were of West Highland or Hebridean origin and originally appear to have been associated with Clan Donald. The name is found in many forms: Cuinn, Suibne, Sweyn, MacCunn, MacSween, MacSuain and MacSwan. In the 13th century there were MacSweens in Argyll at Castle Sween, and the name remained in Argyll in the form of Swene and Macqueen for three or four hundred years. Macqueens, MacSwans and MacSweens are numerous in Skye and Lewis, and Macqueens held the lands of Garafad in Skye for several centuries.

Early in the 15th century, when Malcolm, 10th chief of the Mackintoshes, married Mora MacDonald of Moidart, the bride was accompanied by several of her clansmen, including Revan Macqueen, who settled in the Mackintosh country and subsequently formed septs of the Clan Chattan. Revan Macqueen fought under Mackintosh at the Battle of Harlaw in 1411.

Macqueens settled in Strathdearn on the River Findhorn, and in the 16th century were in possession of the lands of Corrybrough. The Clan Chattan Bond of 1609 was signed by Donald Macqueen of Corrybrough for himself and taking full burden of John Macqueen in Little Corrybrough and Sween Macqueen in Raigbeg. The lands of Corrybrough passed out of the possession of the Macqueens in the 18th century. Robert Macqueen, Lord Braxfield, an eminent if brutal 18th-century lawyer, was of a Lanarkshire family of Macqueens.

Macrae

Crest Badge: *A dexter hand grasping a sword, all proper.*

Motto: *Fortitudine*
(With fortitude).

Gaelic Name: *MacRath.*

The name Macrae, in Gaelic MacRath, 'son of Grace', is supposed to be of ecclesiastical origin. The clan appears to have inhabited the lands of Clunes in the Beauly district in the 12th and 13th centuries and removed to Kintail in the 14th century. The founder of the Kintail branch is said to have been Fionnla Dubh MacGillechriosd, who died in 1416. Duncan, 5th of Kintail, was granted the lands of Inverinate about 1557, and these remained in the family for over 200 years. In 1677, Alexander, eldest son of the Reverend John Macrae of Dingwall, received a 'wadset', or mortgage, of the lands of Conchra and Ardachy and became the progenitor of the Macraes of Conchra.

The Macraes were loyal followers of the MacKenzies, Lords of Kintail and Earls of Seaforth, whose importance owed not a little to Macrae help. At various dates, Macraes were constables of Eilean Donan Castle, and chamberlains and vicars of Kintail. The Reverend Farquhar Macrae, born at Eilean Donan in 1580, was a man of influence and importance, and his grandson, Donnachadh nam Pios, 'Duncan of the Silver Cups', was the compiler of the Fernaig Manuscript, an important collection of Gaelic verse made between 1688 and 1693.

The Macraes took a prominent part in the Civil Wars and were conspicuous for their bravery at Sheriffmuir in 1715. They were not out as a clan in the 1745 Rising, but many individuals took part.

Matheson

Crest Badge: *Out of an eastern crown, or, a naked arm holding a drawn sword, proper.*

Motto: *Fac et spera (Do and hope).*

Gaelic Name: *MacMhathain.*

The Gaelic Manuscript of 1450 derives the Clan MacMathan, or Matheson, from the same source as the MacKenzies, and as in 1427 the chief of the Mathesons is reported to have had 2,000 men, the Clan Matheson was then as powerful as the more famous MacKenzies.

The clan was divided into two main branches, those of Lochalsh in Wester Ross and those of Shiness in Sutherland. Of the former was John Dubh Matheson, who was Constable of Eilean Donan Castle when Donald Gorm of Sleat attacked it in 1539 and both leaders were killed by the opposing force. From John Dubh's son, Murchadh Buidhe of Fernaig and Balmacara are descended the families of Bennetsfield, Iomaire and Glas-na-Muclach.

The Mathesons of Sutherland were an offshoot from the Lochalsh family and are mentioned in the 15th century. They are represented by the Mathesons of Shiness, Achany and the Lews.

John Matheson of the Lochalsh family purchased Attadale in 1730. John, 4th of Attadale, married Margaret, daughter of Donald Matheson of Shiness, and their son Alexander, born, in 1805, was the first baronet of Lochalsh. Sir Alexander made a large fortune in the Far East as one of the founders of Jardine Matheson, and on his return he purchased extensive estates in Ross-shire.

James Sutherland Matheson of the Shiness family purchased the island of Lewis in 1844 and was made a baronet in 1851.

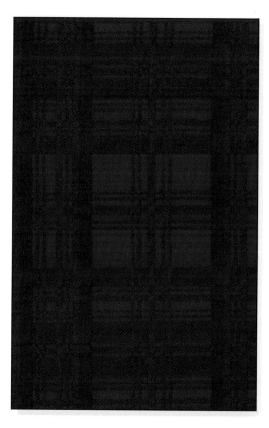

Maxwell

Crest Badge: *A stag lodged in front of a holly bush proper.*

Motto: *Reviresco
(I flourish again).*

The name Maxwell originates in the Borders and means Maccus's 'wiel' or pool, in the River Tweed. In the 13th century Maxwells were sheriffs of Peebles and chamberlains of Scotland. From Herbert and John, two sons of Sir Aymer Maxwell, Chamberlain in 1241, are descended many prominent Maxwell families.

Herbert Maxwell of Caerlaverock in Dumfriesshire, descendant of the first Herbert, was made Lord Maxwell about 1445. John, 3rd Lord, was killed at Flodden in 1513. In 1581, John, 8th Lord, was created Earl of Morton. He was denounced as a rebel but pardoned and eventually killed in a fray with the Johnstons in 1592. In 1608, in revenge for his father's death, his son, the 9th Lord, slew Sir James Johnston. He escaped arrest and fled Scotland but later returned and was executed in 1613.

His brother Robert, who succeeded him, was created Earl of Nithsdale in 1620. The 2nd Earl supported Montrose in 1644 and was succeeded in 1667 by his cousin John, 4th Lord Herries. The 5th Earl joined the Jacobite Rising of 1715, was captured at Preston and sentenced to death for high treason. Aided by his wife, Winifred, who changed clothes with him, he escaped from the Tower of London and died in Rome in 1746. The earldom was forfeited in 1716 but his great-grandson, William Constable-Maxwell, proved his claim to the Lordship of Herries in 1858, but in 1908 it devolved upon the Duchess of Norfolk.

Menzies

Crest Badge: *A savage head affronté,
              erased, proper.*

Motto: *Vill God I Zall
              (Will God I shall).*

Gaelic Name: *Méinn, Méinnearach.*

The name is of Norman descent and found in various forms -
Menzies, Mengues, Mingies and Meyners. It appears in charters
in the 12th and 13th centuries, and in 1249 Robert de
Menyers was Lord High Chamberlain. His son, Alexander,
possessed the lands of Durisdeer in Dumfriesshire, and Weem,
Aberfeldy and Glendochart in Perthshire, which passed to his
son Robert, while his lands in Fortingall passed to his son
Thomas.

At Bannockburn, the Menzies supported Bruce who granted
several charters of lands to members of the clan. David Menzies
was appointed Governor of Orkney and Shetland in 1423
under the King of Norway. In 1487 Sir Robert de Mengues
received a grant of land erected into the barony of Menzies. A
century later, in 1587, the 'Menyessis, in Athoill and Apnadull'
appear in the Roll of the Clans. Sir Alexander Menzies of
Castle Menzies was created a Baronet of Nova Scotia in 1665
for his contributions to that colony, and the baronetcy
continued until the death of Sir Neil, 8th Baronet, in 1910.

A distinguished branch of the clan were the Menzies of
Pitfoddels. At the Battle of Carbisdale in 1650, young Menzies
of Pitfoddels carried the Royal Standard against the
Covenanters. This branch has died out, the last chieftain, John
Menzies, founding Blairs College seminary.

Menzies of Culdares is said to have introduced the first larches
into Scotland from the Tyrol in 1738.

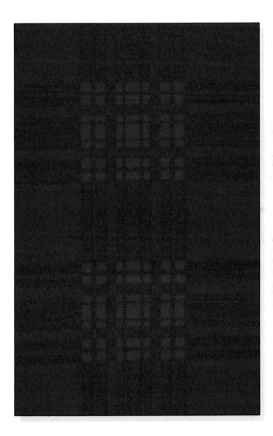

Montgomery

Crest Badge: *A female figure proper, antiquely attired, argent, holding in dexter an anchor or, in sinister a savage's head held by the hair, couped of the fist.*

Motto: *Gardez bien (Look well).*

Gaelic Name: *MacGumerait.*

The Montgomerys are a Lowland clan of Anglo-Norman origin. Roger de Montgomery, a Regent of Normandy, followed William the Conqueror to England, where he was created Earl of Arundel. His grandson, Robert de Montgomery, came to Scotland in the train of Walter, the first High Steward of Scotland in the reign of David I. Robert, who received the manor of Eaglesham, for long the principal home of the Montgomerys, witnessed the foundation charter of the monastery of Paisley in 1160.

Sir John Montgomery, 9th of Eaglesham, distinguished himself at the Battle of Otterburn in 1388 by capturing Sir Henry Percy, called Hotspur. With Percy's ransom, Montgomery built Polnoon Castle. He married Elizabeth de Eglinton and obtained the lands of Eglinton and Ardrossan. Sir Alexander Montgomery was Governor of Kintyre and Knapdale in 1430, and in 1444 was created Lord Montgomery. Hugh, 3rd Lord Montgomery, was created Earl of Eglinton in 1507. Hugh, 5th Earl, died without issue, and the earldom passed to his cousin, Sir Alexander Seton, who took the name and arms of Montgomery.

During the Plantation of Ulster at the end of the 16th century, Lady Montgomery of Eglinton set up linen and woollen manufactures in Ireland.

Morrison

Crest Badge: *Issuant from waves of the sea azure crested argent, a mount vert, thereon an embattled wall azure, masoned argent, and issung therefrom a cubit arm naked proper, the hand grasping a dagger hilted or.*

Motto: *Castle Eistein.*

Gaelic Name: *MacGhille Mhoire.*

According to tradition, the Clan Morrison is said to be of Norse origin, descended from a family which was shipwrecked on the shores of the island of Lewis and saved by clinging to driftwood.

Certainly, the Morrisons were one of the ancient clans of Lewis, and for a long period the Morrisons of Habost held the office of 'brieve' or judge and were known as Clann-na-breitheamh. Hugh Morrison was brieve during the latter half of the 16th century. He was accused by the government of harbouring rebels, and his son John incurred the displeasure of the MacLeods for betraying Torquil Dubh MacLeod, who was beheaded by the MacKenzies in 1597. The Morrisons in consequence had to take refuge on the Scottish mainland, and as many as sixty families are said to have fled to Sutherland. On the abolition of the brieveship in the 17th century, the Morrisons gravitated to the church, and many of their number became prominent clergymen.

A branch of the clan in Harris were celebrated smiths and armourers, and one of this family was the Gaelic poet, John Morrison (1790-1852).

Munro

Crest Badge: *An eagle displayed wings inverted, proper.*

Motto: *Dread God.*

Gaelic Name: *Mac an Rothaich.*

Easter Ross has always been the home of the Munroes. It is claimed that the first Munro of Foulis was Hugh, who died in 1126. About a century later, George Munro of Foulis had a charter from the Earl of Sutherland. Robert, who had a charter from Bruce, led his clan at the Battle of Bannockburn. Robert, 8th of Foulis, married a niece of Euphame, daughter of the Earl of Ross and queen of Robert II. William, 12th of Foulis, knighted by James IV, died in 1505, and Robert Mor, 15th chief, was a staunch supporter of Mary Queen of Scots. He received many favours from her son, James VI.

During the 17th century, the Munros engaged actively in the European wars, and Robert, 18th chief, joined the army of Gustavus Adolphus. He raised 700 men of his own clan for service in Sweden and greatly distinguished himself there, where the Scots received the name of 'The Invincibles'. At that time there were 'Three generals, eight colonels, five lieut-colonels, eleven majors, and above thirty captains, all of the name of Monroe'.

Sir Robert Munro, 6th Baronet, commanded the Black Watch at the Battle of Fontenoy in 1745, when, using their own method of fighting - alternately firing and taking cover - for the first time in a European battle they introduced a system of infantry tactics that was not superseded.

On the death of the 11th Baronet, inheritance passed through his eldest daughter.

Murray

Crest Badge: *A mermaid holding in her dexter hand a mirror, and in the sinister a comb all proper.*

Motto: *Tout prêt (Quite ready).*

Gaelic Name: *MacMhuirich.*

This powerful clan had its origin in one of the ancient Pictish tribes of the Province of Moray. The clan name is found in many districts of Scotland, and the principal family is said to be descended from Freskin, who received lands in Moray from David I. His grandson, William, was described as de Móravia. He acquired the lands of Bothwell and others in the south of Scotland, and several of his sons founded other houses. He died in 1226, and his son, Sir Walter, was the first described as of Bothwell. Sir Walter was succeeded by his brother, Sir Andrew, a celebrated patriot who organized a rising in Moray and fought with William Wallace to defeat the English at the Battle of Stirling Bridge in 1297, where he was probably killed. His son, also Sir Andrew, was regent of Scotland after the death of Robert the Bruce in 1329.

In 1282, Sir William de Moravia acquired through marriage the lands of Tullibardine in Perthshire. Sir William Murray of Tullibardine, who succeeded in 1446, had seventeen sons, many of whom founded prominent families of Murray. Sir John, 12th of Tullibardine, was created Lord Murray in 1604 and Earl of Tullibardine in 1606. William, 2nd Earl, claimed the earldom of Atholl by right of his wife but died before it was granted. His son, John obtained the title in 1629 and became the 1st Murray Earl of Atholl. His son, William, a prominent Jacobite, forfeited the title to his brother.

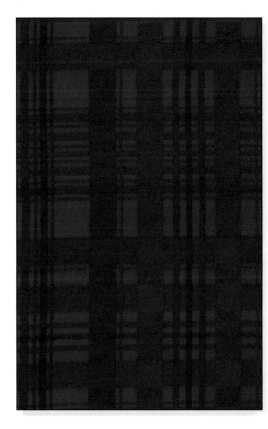

Murray of Atholl

Crest Badge: *A mermaid holding in her dexter hand a mirror, and in the sinister a comb all proper.*

Motto: *Tout prêt (Quite ready).*

Gaelic Name: *MacMhuirich.*

John, 1st Earl of Atholl of the Murray branch, obtained the title in 1629, and the earldom of Tullibardine was conferred on his uncle, Sir Patrick Murray. Atholl was a staunch royalist, and his son John, 2nd Earl, strongly supported Charles I. In 1670 he succeeded to the earldom of Tullibardine, and in 1676 he was created Marquis of Atholl. Disappointed at his reception by William of Orange, he joined the Jacobites. He died in 1703. John, 2nd Marquis, was created Duke of Atholl in 1703 and was a bitter opponent of the Union of 1707. He died in 1724 and was succeeded by his third son, James. John's first son predeceased him, and his second son, William, with his brothers Charles and George, were engaged in the Jacobite Risings of 1715, 1719 and 1745. Lord George, who unfurled Prince Charles' standard at Glenfinnan, was the brilliant Lieutenant-General of the Prince's army.

As his son and eldest daughter died young, James 2nd Duke of Atholl was succeeded by his daughter Charlotte, who married her cousin, John Murray, eldest son of Lord George Murray of Jacobite fame. John Murray succeeded his uncle as 3rd Duke of Atholl and holder of many other titles of the Murray family. Other branches of the clan include the Murrays of Polmaise, of Abercairney, of Auchtertyre, of Elibank, and many others, the Earls of Dunmore and the Earls of Mansfield.

Napier

Crest Badge: *A cubit arm, the hand grasping a crescent argent.*

Motto: *Sans tache*
(Without stain).

Originally an English name, the Napier having charge of the royal linen, according to tradition, the Scottish Napiers were descended from the ancient Earls of Lennox, and John de Napier, who held lands in the county of Dunbarton, is recorded in a charter of the Earls of Lennox in 1280. He is also recorded in the Ragman Rolls of 1296, and he assisted in the defence of Stirling Castle in 1303. A descendant of his, William de Napier, was governor of Edinburgh Castle in 1402. William's son, Alexander, who owned the lands of Merchiston, was provost of Edinburgh in 1437, and his son, Sir Alexander Napier of Merchiston, held a number of important posts, including that of Ambassador to England in 1461.

Archibald Napier of Merchiston obtained Gartness, Rusky and other lands in 1509. His son, Alexander, was killed at Flodden in 1513, and the latter's son was killed at Pinkie in 1547. John Napier of Merchiston, born in 1550, was the discoverer of logarithms and considered a great mathematician. His son, Sir Archibald, was a Lord of Session and was created Baron Napier of Merchiston in 1627. He was a strong supporter of Charles I, and his son, Archibald, 2nd Lord, fought with Montrose. Archibald, 3rd Lord Napier, died a bachelor and the titles passed through the female line to the Scotts of Thirlestane. Francis, 5th Lord Napier, was the grandfather of Admiral Sir Charles Napier, a distinguished British naval commander.

Ogilvie

Crest Badge: *A woman naked from the waist up draped azure pinned or holding a portcullis gules.*

Motto: *À fin (To the end).*

Gaelic Name: *Mac Ghille Bhuidhe.*

The Ogilvies take their name from Gilbert, a descendant of the ancient Earls of Angus, who was granted the barony of Ogilvie by William the Lion about 1163. In 1392, Sir Walter Ogilvie of Auchterhouse was killed in a battle with the Clann Donnachaidh, the Clan Robertson. His son, the Sheriff of Angus, styled Lord Ogilvie, was killed at the Battle of Harlaw in 1411. Sir Walter, son of the Sheriff, was Lord High Treasurer and built the tower of Airlie.

Sir James Ogilvie of Airlie was created Lord Ogilvie of Airlie in 1491. The Ogilvies were royalists during the Civil Wars, and James, 1st Earl of Airlie, gave gallant service to the cause. James, 2nd Earl, taken prisoner at Philiphaugh in 1645 and sentenced to death, escaped from the Castle of St Andrews on the eve of his execution, dressed in his sister's clothes. The Ogilvies engaged actively in the Jacobite Risings of 1715 and 1745. David, 5th Lord Ogilvie, son of John, 4th Earl of Airlie, who joined Prince Charles with the Clan Ogilvie, was attainted and fled to France. Receiving a free pardon, he returned in 1783 and died in 1813. His son, Walter Ogilvie of Airlie, assumed the title of 7th Earl in 1812, but it was not restored until 1825 when his son David was confirmed in it by Act of Parliament. David, 8th Earl of Airlie, was killed at the Battle of Diamond Hill in South Africa in 1900.

Oliphant and Melville

Crest Badge: *Unicorn couped argent, crined and armed, or.*

Motto: *A tout pourvoir (Provide for all).*

David de Olifard, who accompanied David I on a journey from Winchester in 1141, is said to be the progenitor of the house of Oliphant. In 1458, the title of Lord Oliphant was conferred on Sir Lawrence Oliphant, a descendant of David de Olifard, and the lands of Gask and Aberdalgie were obtained from Robert I. From Sir Lawrence's second son, William, the Oliphants of Gask were descended, while his third son, George, was styled of Bachilton.

The Oliphants of Gask were ardent Jacobites, and Lawrence Oliphant of Gask and his eldest son were attainted for their participation in the Rising of 1745. The Scottish poet, Lady Nairne, born Carolina Oliphant, was of the Gask family and named Carolina in honour of Prince Charles. On the death of the 11th Lord in 1751, the title became dormant.

The Melvilles are a Lothian family, the first settling in Scotland during the reign of David I. He called his manor 'Mala Ville', hence Melville. Early on, the Melvilles held many important offices under the Crown. Eventually the family died out, and the Barony of Melville came into the family of Ross of Halkhead through marriage with the Melville heiress. The title Earl of Melville was conjoined with that of the Earl of Leven. The tartan shown here was for long known under the trade name of 'Oliphant and Melville'. A different pattern under the name Melville is found in some early collections of tartan.

Ramsay

Crest Badge: *A unicorn's head, couped, argent, armed and crined, or.*

Motto: *Ora et labora (Pray and work).*

Gaelic Name: *Ramsaidh.*

The Ramsays are an ancient family of Anglo-Norman origin. The first of the name recorded in Scotland was Simon de Ramsay who was granted lands in Lothian by David I. He was the ancestor of the Ramsays of Dalhousie. The names of many of the family appear in charters prior to 1296 when that of William de Ramsay appears in the Ragman Rolls. He later supported Bruce and in 1320 signed the letter to the Pope asserting the independence of Scotland.

During the next three centuries the Ramsays were prominently engaged in the Border wars. In 1618, George Ramsay of Dalhousie was created Lord Ramsay of Melrose, a title changed a few months later to Lord Ramsay of Dalhousie. His son, William, was created Earl of Dalhousie by Charles I in 1633. During the War of the Spanish Succession, William, 5th Earl, was colonel of the Scots Guards sent to support Archduke Charles of Austria. He died in Spain in 1710. George, 9th Earl, a distinguished military man, in 1815 was created Baron Dalhousie in the peerage of the United Kingdom. His son, James, 10th Earl, was created Marquess of Dalhousie in 1849. He was Governor-General of India from 1847 until 1855. When he died in 1860, the title of Marquess became extinct. The Scottish titles of Earl of Dalhousie and Baron Ramsay devolved on his cousin Fox, 2nd Lord Panmure, 11th Earl of Dalhousie. The Ramsays of Bamff, Perthshire, are descended from Adam de Ramsay of Bamff, a 13th-century baron.

Robertson

Crest Badge: *A dexter hand holding an imperial crown, all proper.*

Motto: *Virtutis gloria merces (Glory is the reward of valour).*

Gaelic Name: *Mac Raibeirt (MacDonnachaidh).*

The Robertsons, known as Clann Donnachaidh, are claimed to be descended from the Celtic Earls of Atholl. The clan takes its Gaelic name from Donnachadh Reamhar, Stout Duncan, the staunch friend of Bruce who led the clan at Bannockburn. It was from Robert Riach, Grizzled Robert, that the clan took the name Robertsons. This Robert was the chief who captured the murderers of James I and delivered them to the government, and for this action he received, in 1451, a Crown charter erecting his lands into the Barony of Struan. About a century later the Earl of Atholl seized about half of the Struan lands under a 'wadset', or mortgage, and the Robertsons never recovered them.

The Robertsons were loyal adherents of the Stuarts and accompanied Montrose in all his campaign, and after the Restoration Charles II settled a pension on Robertson of Struan. Alexander, the celebrated poet, chief of Struan, born about 1670, was studying for the church when he succeeded to the chiefship, but he left the cloisters and joined Dundee in 1688. He was attainted but received a remission in 1703. He was out again in 1715 and was captured at Sheriffmuir but escaped to France. He was pardoned in 1731 but joined Prince Charles in 1745 with the clan. He was then too old to fight, however, and returned home in Sir John Cope's carriage. He died in 1749.

Rose

Crest Badge: *A harp, azure.*

Motto: *Constant and true.*

Gaelic Name: *Ròs, Ròis.*

The Clan Rose were settled in the district of Nairn in the 12th century, and there is documentary evidence to prove that about 1219 Hugh Rose of Geddes was witness to the foundation charter of Beauly Priory. His son Hugh acquired the lands of Kilravock on the Moray Firth by marriage, and Kilravock remains with the family to the present day. In 1433, John Rose, 6th of Kilravock, received confirmation of his lands from James I. His son Hugh built the old tower of Kilravock in 1460. The Barony of Kilravock was erected in 1474. Hugh, 10th of Kilravock, was taken prisoner at the Battle of Pinkie in 1547. He was Sheriff of Ross, Constable of Inverness Castle, and Sheriff Principal of Inverness. He died in 1597, aged 90.

The Roses of Kilravock were loyal to the government during the Jacobite Risings of 1715 and 1745. Hugh, 15th of Kilravock, Sheriff of Ross, voted against the Union of 1707 but was one of the commissioners to represent Scotland in the first British parliament.

Sir Hugh H. Rose, born in 1803, was in command of the Central Field Force during the Indian Mutiny, in the course of which he fought sixteen successful actions, captured 150 pieces of artillery, took twenty forts and captured Ratghur, Shanghur, Chundehree, Jhansi and Calpee. He was raised to the peerage as Baron Strathnairn in 1866 and was made Field Marshal in 1877. Kilravock Castle is still inhabited by the chief of the clan.

Ross

Crest Badge: *A dexter hand holding a garland of laurel, all proper.*

Motto: *Spem successus alit (Success nourishes hope).*

Gaelic Name: *Ròs, Ròis.*

The Clan Ross take their name from the ancient province of Ross and are designated in Gaelic as Clann Andrias. Their traditional progenitor Fearchar Mac-an-t-sagairt, 'son of the priest', of Applecross, was a powerful supporter of Alexander II, and for his services was created Earl of Ross about 1234. His grandson, William, led his clan at the Battle of Bannockburn, and Hugh, 5th Earl, was killed at the Battle of Halidon Hill in 1333. Hugh's successor, William, died without male issue, and succession passed through the female line, a circumstance which later led to the struggle for the earldom between the Lord of the Isles and Regent Albany. In 1424, the earldom reverted to the Crown, but James I restored it to Margaret, mother of Alexander, 3rd Lord of the Isles, and it remained with the Lords of the Isles until the Lordship was forfeited in 1476, when the earldom became vested in the Crown.

On the death of William, Earl of Ross, the chiefship of the clan passed to his brother Hugh Ross of Rariches, who obtained a charter of the lands of Balnagowan in 1374. David Ross, the last of the direct line of Balnagowan, settled the estate on the Hon. Charles Ross, son of Lord Ross of Hawkhead, Renfrewshire. Balnagowan devolved upon George, 13th Lord Ross, in 1745. On the death of the unmarried 14th Lord Ross, Balnagowan went to Sir James Lockhart, 2nd Baronet of Carstairs.

Scott

Crest Badge: *A stag trippant, proper, attired and unguled, or.*

Motto: *Amo (I love).*

Gaelic Name: *Scot, Scotach.*

The Scotts, one of the most powerful Border clans, take their name from a race who invaded Scotland at an early date and filtered into many other countries. Uchtredus filius Scoti witnessed charters between 1107 and 1128, and from him were descended the Scotts of Buccleuch and the Scotts of Balwearie. The Buccleuchs exchanged Murdochston in Lanarkshire for Branxholm in Roxburghshire. Sir Walter, 13th Baron, was created Lord Scott of Buccleuch by James VI, and his son was raised to the earldom of Buccleuch in 1619. On the failure of the male line, Anna, Countess of Buccleuch, married James, Duke of Monmouth, natural son of Charles II, who was created Duke of Buccleuch. His grandson became 2nd Duke, and the 3rd Duke succeeded to the dukedom of Queensberry. Sir Michael Scott, knighted by Alexander II, obtained the lands of Balwearie by marriage with the heiress of Sir Richard Balwearie. His putative son, Sir Michael, who died about 1300, was an astrologer and wizard, who was said to have split the Eildon Hills in three but was actually a most learned man. Of fourteen successive barons of Balwearie, thirteen were knighted. The Balwearie family are now represented by the Scotts of Ancrum.

Sir Walter Scott, the famous Scottish writer, was a descendant of the Scotts of Harden, one of the many prominent families of the clan.

Shaw

Crest Badge: *A dexter arm, the hand holding a dagger in pale proper.*

Motto: *Fide et fortitudine (By fidelity and fortitude).*

Gaelic Name: *Mac Ghille-Sheathanaich.*

Clan Shaw was one of the principal clans of the confederation of Clan Chattan. Farquhart Shaw, Shaw Mor, great-grandson of Angus, 6th Chief of Mackintosh and Eva of Clan Chattan was, by tradition, the leader of Clan Chattan at the clan battle on the North Inch in Perth in 1396. The lands of Rothiemurchus were given to him as a reward, but they were sold in the 16th century. His son, James, was killed at Harlaw in 1411, but his heir, Alasdair Ciar, succeeded him.

Alasdair's brother, Adam (Ay) of Tordarroch, was founder of Clan Ay. Tordarroch acted for Clan Shaw after 1539, and at Inverness in 1543 and Termit in 1609 signed the Clan Chattan Bands. The Shaws supported Montrose and raised the Shaw contingent in the Jacobite Rising of 1715.

Alasdair's second son, Alexander, was ancestor of the Shaws of Dell; his third, James, of the Shaws of Dalnavert; his fourth, Farquhar, was progenitor of Clan Farquharson; and the fifth, Iver, ancestor of the Shaws of Harris and the Isles.

The Shaws of the Lowlands have their origins with William de Shaw, whose name appears in the Ragman Rolls of 1296. The Shaws of Sauchie and the Shaws of Greenock were important branches of the family.

A new chief of Clan Shaw, the 21st, matriculated in 1970 after a vacancy of 400 years. Tordarroch in Strathnairn is still held.

Sinclair

Crest Badge: *A cock, proper armed and beaked or.*

Motto: *Commit thy work to God.*

Gaelic Name: *Mac na Ceardadh.*

Of Norman origin, the first of the name was William de Sancto Claro, who received a grant of the barony of Roslin, Midlothian, in the 12th century. Sir Henry St Clair of Roslin supported Robert the Bruce, and his son, Sir William, accompanied Sir James Douglas on his journey to the Holy Land with the heart of Bruce and died fighting the Moors in Spain.

In 1379, Henry, son of Sir William Sinclair, obtained the earldom of Orkney through his father's marriage with Isabella, Countess of Orkney. William, 3rd Earl, founded Roslin Chapel in 1446, and received the earldom of Caithness in 1455. In 1470, the earldom of Orkney, which had been held from King Haco, was purchased from the Sinclairs by James III. The Earls of Caithness were engaged in a long succession of feuds with the Sutherlands, the Gunns, and other clans, and George, 6th Earl, deeply in debt, granted a disposition of his title and estates to Sir John Campbell of Glenorchy. The Earl died without issue, and Campbell took possession of the estates in 1676. His claim to the title was disputed by George Sinclair of Keiss. In 1680, the Campbells defeated the Sinclairs in battle, but Sinclair's claim to the title was established in 1681.

The many prominent families of Sinclairs include the Sinclairs of Ulbster, but the Sinclairs of Argyll and the West of Scotland, known as Clann na Cearda, or 'craftsmen', do not appear to be connected with the Sinclairs of the north.

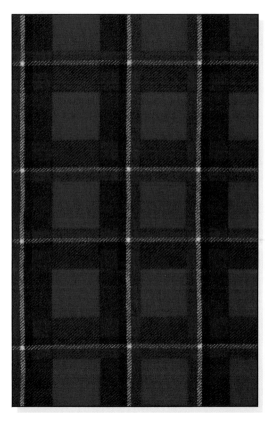

Skene

Crest Badge: *A dexter arm embowed, issuing from a cloud, hand holding a laurel wreath, all proper.*

Motto: *Virtutis regia merces (A palace the reward of bravery).*

Gaelic Name: *MacSgian.*

The traditional origin of the Clan Skene takes us back to the 11th century, when a younger son of Robertson of Struan saved the life of the king by killing a wolf with his sgian and was rewarded with the lands of Skene in Aberdeenshire.

John de Skene signed the Ragman Rolls of 1296. His grandson, Robert, was a faithful follower of Robert the Bruce, from whom he received a charter erecting the lands of Skene into a barony. The chiefs were unfortunate in battle. In 1411 Adam de Skene was killed at Harlaw, Alexander fell at Flodden in 1513, and his grandson, another Alexander, was killed at Pinkie in 1547. James Skene of Skene supported the royalist cause during the reign of Charles I, and later served in the army of Gustavus Adolphus of Sweden. In 1827 the family of Skene of Skene died out in the direct line, and the estates passed to James, 4th Earl of Fife, nephew of the last Skene of Skene. Other prominent families of Skenes included those of Dyce, Halyards, Cariston, Curriehill and Rubislaw. Sir John Skene, a celebrated lawyer, was admitted a Lord of Session in 1594 and took the title Lord Curriehill.

William Forbes Skene, the celebrated writer on Scots-Celtic history, was born in 1809. He was appointed Historiographer Royal for Scotland in 1881 and died in 1892.

Stewart

Crest Badge: *A pelican argent winged or feeding its young proper. (The crest shown here is that of the Earl of Galloway).*

Motto: *Virescit vulnere virtus (Courage grows strong at a wound).*

Gaelic Name: *Stiubhard.*

The Stewarts are descended from Walter, the son of an Anglo-Norman baron, who came to Scotland in the 12th century and who was appointed High Steward of the royal household by David I. Walter also received lands in Renfrew, Paisley, Pollok, Cathcart, and elsewhere. The office of High Steward was made hereditary to the family by Malcolm IV. James, 5th High Steward, bravely supported Sir William Wallace and Robert the Bruce in their struggle for Scottish independence. Walter, 6th High Steward, married Princess Marjory, daughter of Robert the Bruce, and from these were descended the royal house of Stewart. The male line of the royal Stewarts ended with the death in 1807 of Prince Henry, Cardinal Duke of York, brother of Prince Charles Edward.

Many noble families were descended from the royal line, and Stewarts have held or hold the dukedoms of Albany, Rothesay, and Lennox, the marquessate of Bute, and the earldoms of Menteith, Angus, Atholl, Strathearn, Carrick, Buchan, and Galloway. Among other Stewart families were those of Bonkyl, Blackhall, and Greenock, Castlemilk, Balquhidder, Achnacone, Ardsheil, Ardvorlich, Dalguise, Fasnacloich, Grandtully, and Invernahyle. The Royal Stewart tartan was always regarded as the personal tartan of the royal house of Scotland, and is now the royal tartan of Her Majesty The Queen.

Stewart of Appin

Crest Badge: *A unicorn's head, crined and armed, or.*

Motto: *Quidder we'll zje (Whither will ye).*

Gaelic Name: *Stiubhard.*

Sir John Stewart of Bonkyl, son of Alexander, High Steward of Scotland, was the ancestor of this West Highland clan. One of his descendants obtained the Lordship of Lorn through marriage to the heiress of Lorn. Sir John Stewart of Lorn was murdered at Dunstaffnage Castle about 1463, and his son Dougal became 1st of Appin. Dougal unsuccessfully tried to recover the Lordship of Lorn.

The clan fought at the Battles of Flodden and Pinkie, in 1513 and 1547. At Pinkie the clan was led by Donald Stewart of Invernahyle, known as Donald nam Ord. In 1645, they supported Montrose at the Battle of Inverlochy and in the same year also fought at Auldearn and Kilsyth. The chief of Appin was outlawed and his lands forfeited, but they were returned to him at the Restoration. The clan joined Dundee's campaign in 1688 and supported the Jacobites in the Risings of 1715 and 1745. After the Battle of Culloden, the banner of the Appin regiment was one of the few saved from destruction.

In 1765, the estate was sold by the 9th chief who was succeeded in the chiefship by his cousin Duncan, 6th of Ardsheil, who became 10th of Appin in 1769. In 1782, the 10th chief obtained the restoration of his confiscated paternal estate of Ardshiel. Castle Stalker, once a stronghold of the Stewarts of Lorn, passed into Campbell possession but was re-acquired by a Stewart.

Sutherland

Crest Badge: *A cat sejant erect guardant proper.*

Motto: *Sans peur (Without fear).*

Gaelic Name: *Sutherlarach.*

The territory lying to the south of Caithness was known to the Norsemen as Sudrland, and doubtless the inhabitants assumed their name from the district. The Earls of Sutherland, who were chiefs of the clan until 1514, are descended from Freskin, the progenitor of the Murrays.

The earldom of Sutherland is claimed to be the oldest in Britain and is alleged to have been granted to William, Lord of Sutherland, in about 1228. William was the great-grandson of Freskin, the ancestor of the Murrays of Atholl. William, 2nd Earl of Sutherland, fought for Bruce at Bannockburn, and his son Kenneth, 3rd Earl, was killed at the Battle of Halidon Hill in 1333. William, 4th Earl, married a daughter of Robert the Bruce. His successors had many feuds with neighbouring clans, particularly the Mackays. John, 9th Earl, died in 1514 without male issue, and the title passed to his sister, whose husband was Adam Gordon of Aboyne.

The Gordon Earls of Sutherland encountered the same inter-clan enmities as their predecessors, and John, 11th Earl, and his Countess were poisoned by Isobel Sinclair at the instigation of the Earl of Caithness. William, 18th Earl, died in 1766, the last of the Gordon Earls of Sutherland. His daughter Elizabeth, Countess of Sutherland in her own right, married George Granville-Leveson-Gower, afterwards Marquis of Stafford, who was created Duke of Sutherland in 1833.

Urquhart

Crest Badge: *Issuing from a crest coronet,
a female naked from waist
up holding in her dexter
hand a sword, and in the
sinister a tree.*

Motto: *Mean, speak and do weil.*

Gaelic Name: *Urchurdan.*

The Urquharts derive their name from the district of Urquhart
in the old sheriffdom of Cromarty, and are of ancient origin.
Sir Thomas Urquhart, who compiled his own genealogy, even
described himself as the 143rd in direct descent from Adam
and Eve.

William Urquhart, Sheriff of Cromarty at the beginning of the
14th century, married a daughter of Hugh, Earl of Ross, and
his son added considerably to the family possessions. Sir
Thomas Urquhart of Cromarty, who married Helen, daughter
of Lord Abernethy, is alleged to have been the father of twenty-
five sons, seven of whom were killed at the Battle of Pinkie in
1547. The eldest son, Alexander, received a charter in 1532
from James V granting him lands in Ross-shire and Inverness-
shire. Alexander's son, John of Craigfintry and Culbo, was
tutor to his grand-nephew, Sir Thomas, and is the 'Tutour of
Cromartie' named in the Roll of Landlords, 1587. Sir Thomas
Urquhart of Cromarty was a 17th-century royalist soldier and
writer, notable chiefly for his translation of Rabelais and for his
epigrams. Colonel James Urquhart, who died in 1741, was the
last of the male line.

The chiefship passed to the Urquharts of Meldrum who are
descended from John, the Tutor of Cromarty. The chiefship
became dormant in 1898 and remained so until 1958 when the
present chief was adjuged heir male and chief by Lyon Court.

Wallace

Crest Badge: *A dexter arm in armour, embowed, in hand a sword, all proper.*

Motto: *Pro libertate (For liberty).*

Gaelic Name: *Uallas.*

In old Latin documents the term Wallensis or Walensis was used to designate the Welsh, but in Scotland it was used more particularly to describe the Britons of Strathclyde who were of the same stock. From this word the name Wallace is derived. In the 12th century, Richard Wallace obtained extensive lands in Ayrshire, in the district now known as Riccarton. His descendant, Sir Malcolm Wallace of Elderslie, was the father of Scotland's greatest patriot, Sir William Wallace, who was his second son.

While still very young, Wallace became the leader of a company of patriots, and his harassing tactics against the English earned him the support of many nobles. His reprisal against the garrison at Lanark for the murder of his sweetheart and the burning of the 'barns of Ayr' in revenge for the murder of his uncle and other gentlemen who had been invited to a conference, gained him still more supporters. His military genius made him hated and feared by Edward I, and his only defeats were brought about by the jealousies and treachery of nobles forming his own armies. By treachery, he was captured at Robroyston, near Glasgow, and delivered to Edward I by Sir John Mentieth. Wallace was brutally executed in London in 1305.

The Wallaces of Craigie, of Cessnock, of Kelly and of Cairnhill were all descended from the original family of Riccarton in Ayrshire.

Clan and Family Names

Clan septs were of two classes: clansmen of the clan who were related by blood and formed separate branches, and individuals and groups who sought and obtained the protection of the clan. This resulted in a clan having septs of different surnames, and also in persons with the same surname being attached to different clans. In the list below, the family name is given first, followed by the clan name with which it is usually associated and whose tartan can be worn by members of that family. Septs which now have tartans of their own are marked with an asterisk (*).

Even respected authorities differ on the complex question of clan and sept associations, therefore this list cannot claim to be fully comprehensive or definitive.

Abbot *Macnab*
Abbotson *Macnab*
Abercrombie*
Abernethy *Leslie*
Adam *Gordon*
Adamson *Mackintosh*
Adie *Gordon*
Airlie *Ogilvie*
Alexander *MacAlister, MacDonald, MacDonell of Glengarry*
Allan *MacDonald of Clanranald, MacFarlane*
Allanson *MacDonald of Clanranald, MacFarlane*
Allardice *Graham of Menteith*

Allison*
Alpin *MacAlpine*
Anderson* *Ross*
Andrew *Ross*
Angus* *MacInnes*
Arthur *MacArthur*
Austin *Keith*
Ayson *Mackintosh*
Baillie*
Bain *MacBean, MacKay, Macnab*
Balneaves *Murray*
Bannatyne *Campbell of Argyll, Stuart of Bute*
Bannerman *Forbes*
Bard *Baird*
Bartholomew *MacFarlane*

Baxter* *Macmillan*
Bayne *MacBean, MacKay, Macnab*
Bean *MacBean*
Beath *MacDonald*
Beaton, *MacDonald, MacLean, MacLeod of Harris*
Begg *MacDonald*
Bell *Macmillan*
Berkeley *Barclay*
Bethune *MacDonald, MacLean, MacLeod of Harris*
Beton *MacDonald, MacLean, MacLeod of Harris*
Binnie *MacBean*
Black *Lamont, MacGregor, MacLean*
Bontein, Bontine, Bunten *Graham of Menteith*
Bowie* *MacDonald*
Boyd* *Stewart (Royal)*
Brebner *Farquharson*
Brewer *Drummond, MacGregor*
Brieve *Morrison*
Brown *Lamont, Macmillan*
Buchan *Cumming*
Burdon *Lamont*
Burk *MacDonald*
Burnett* *Campbell*
Burns* *Campbell*
Caddell *Campbell of Cawdor*
Caird *MacGregor, Sinclair*
Calder *Campbell of Cawdor*

Callum *MacLeod of Raasay, Campbell, MacArthur*
Cariston *Skene*
Carmichael* *MacDougall, Stewart of Appin*
Carnegie*
Carson *Macpherson*
Cattanach *Macpherson*
Caw *MacFarlane*
Chalmers *Cameron*
Cheyne *Sutherland*
Christie* *Farquharson*
Clanachan *MacLean*
Clark, Clerk* *Cameron, Mackintosh, Macpherson*
Clarke *Cameron*
Clarkson *Cameron, Mackintosh, Macpherson*
Clyne *Sinclair*
Cochrane*
Cockburn*
Collier *Robertson*
Colman *Buchanan*
Colson *MacDonald*
Colyear *Robertson*
Combich *Stewart of Appin*
Combie *Mackintosh*
Comrie *MacGregor*
Conacher *MacDougall*
Connall*, Conn *MacDonald*
Conochie *Campbell*
Cook *Stewart*
Coulson *MacDonald*
Coutts *Farquharson*
Cowan *Colquhoun, MacDougall*

Cranston*
Crauford, Crawford* *Lindsay*
Crerar *Mackintosh*
Crombie *MacDonald*
Crookshanks *Stewart*
Cruickshanks *Stewart*
Currie *MacDonald of Clanranald, Macpherson*
Dallas *Mackintosh*
Dalziel*
Darroch *MacDonald*
Davie *Davidson*
Davis, Davison *Davidson*
Dawson *Davidson*
Denoon *Campbell*
Deuchar *Lindsay*
Dewar *Macnab, Menzies*
Dinnes *Innes*
Dingwall *Munro, Ross*
Dis, Dise *Skene*
Dochart *MacGregor*
Doig *Drummond*
Doles *Mackintosh*
Donachie *Robertson*
Donald *MacDonald*
Donaldson *MacDonald*
Donleavy *Buchanan*
Dougall *MacDougall*
Dove *Buchanan*
Dow *Buchanan, Davidson*
Dowall, Dowell *MacDougall*
Drysdale *Douglas*
Duff *MacDuff*
Duffie, Duffy *Macfie*
Dullach *Stewart*
Dunbar*

Duncan* *Robertson*
Duncanson *Duncan*
Dunnachie *Robertson*
Dyce* *Skene*
Edie *Gordon*
Elder *Mackintosh*
Ennis *Innes*
Errol *Hay*
Esson *Shaw*
Ewan, Ewen *MacEwen*
Ewing *MacEwen*
Fair *Ross*
Farquhar *Farquharson*
Federith *Sutherland*
Fergus *Ferguson*
Ferries *Ferguson*
Ferson *Macpherson*
Fife *MacDuff*
Findlay, Finlay, Findlayson *Farquharson*
Findlater *Ogilvie*
Fleming *Murray*
Fordyce *Forbes*
Forsyth*
Foulis *Munro*
France *Stewart*
Fresell, Friseal, Frizell *Fraser*
Frew *Fraser*
Fullerton *Stuart of Bute*
Fyfe *MacDuff*
Galbraith* *MacDonald, MacFarlane*
Gallie *Gunn*
Garrow *Stewart*
Garvie *MacLean*
Gaunson *Gunn*

Geddes *Gordon*
Georgeson *Gunn*
Gibb, Gibson *Buchanan*
Gilbert *Buchanan*
Gilbertson *Buchanan*
Gilbride *MacDonald*
Gilchrist *MacLachlan,*
  Ogilvie
Gilfillan *Macnab*
Gillanders *Ross*
Gillespie *Macpherson*
Gillies* *Macpherson*
Gilmore *Morrison*
Gilroy *Grant, MacGillivray*
Gladstone*
Glen, Glennie *Mackintosh*
Gorrie *MacDonald*
Gow* *Macpherson*
Gowrie *MacDonald*
Gray *Stewart, Sutherland*
Gregor, Grigor *MacGregor*
Gregorson *MacGregor*
Gregory *MacGregor*
Greig *MacGregor*
Grewar, Gruer *MacGregor*
Grier *MacGregor*
Grierson *MacGregor*
Haig*
Hallyard *Skene*
Hanna, Hannah *Hannay*
Hardie, Hardy
  Farquharson, Mackintosh
Harper *Buchanan*
Harperson *Buchanan*
Harris *Campbell*
Hastings *Campbell*

Hawes, Hawson *MacTavish*
Hawthorn *MacDonald*
Hendrie, Hendry *Henderson,*
  MacNaughton
Hewison *MacDonald*
Home*
Houston *MacDonald*
Howison *MacDonald*
Hughson *MacDonald*
Hunter*
Huntly *Gordon*
Hutcheson *MacDonald*
Hutchinson *MacDonald*
Hutchison *MacDonald*
Inches *Robertson*
Inglis*
Innie *Innes*
Irvine*
Jameson *Gunn, Stuart of Bute*
Jardine*
Johnson* *Gunn, MacDonald*
Kay *Davidson*
Kean, Keene *Gunn,*
  MacDonald
Kellie, Kelly *MacDonald*
Kendrick *Henderson,*
  MacNaughton
Kenneth *MacKenzie*
Kennethson *MacKenzie*
Kilgour*
Kilpatrick *Colquhoun*
King *MacGregor*
Kinnell *MacDonald*
Kinnieson* *MacFarlane*
Kirkpatrick *Colquhoun*
Lachlan *MacLachlan*

Lamb, Lambie, Lammie *Lamont*
Lammond, Lamondson *Lamont*
Landers *Lamont*
Lang *MacDonald*
Lauchlan *MacLachlan*
Lauder*
Laurence *MacLaren*
Law *MacLaren*
Lawrie *MacLaren*
Lean *MacLean*
Leckie, Lecky *MacGregor*
Lees *Macpherson*
Lemond *Lamont*
Lennie, Lenny *Buchanan*
Lennox* *MacFarlane, Stewart*
Lewis *MacLeod of Lewis*
Limond, Limont *Lamont*
Linklater *Sinclair*
Lobban *Logan*
Loudoun *Campbell*
Love *MacKinnon*
Low *MacLaren*
Lucas *Lamont*
Luke *Lamont*
Lumsden* *Forbes*
Lyall *Sinclair*
Lyon *Farquharson*
MacAdam *MacGregor*
MacAdie *Munro*
MacAlaster *MacAlister*
Macalduie *Lamont*
MacAlester *MacAlister*
MacAllan *MacDonald of*

Clanranald, *MacFarlane*
Macandeoir *Buchanan, Macnab, Menzies*
MacAndrew (*see* Anderson), *Mackintosh, Ross*
MacAngus *MacInnes*
Macara *MacGregor, Macrae*
Macaree *MacGregor*
MacAskill *MacLeod of Harris*
MacAslan, MacAuslan, MacAusland *Buchanan*
MacAy *Mackintosh*
MacBain *MacBean*
MacBeth* *MacBean, MacDonald, MacLean*
MacBrayne *MacNaughton*
MacBride *MacDonald*
MacBrieve *Morrison*
MacCaig *Farquharson, MacLeod of Harris*
MacCainsh *MacInnes*
MacCall *MacColl*
MacCalmont *Buchanan*
MacCamie *Stewart*
MacCammon, MacCammond *Buchanan*
MacCansh *MacInnes*
MacCardney *Farquharson, Mackintosh*
MacCarter *MacArthur*
MacCash *MacDonald*
MacCaskill *MacLeod*
MacCaul *MacDonald, MacColl*
MacCause *MacFarlane*
MacCaw *Stewart*
MacCay *MacKay*

MacClerich, MacChlery *Cameron, Mackintosh, Macpherson*
MacCloy *Stuart of Bute*
MacClure *MacLeod*
MacClymont *Lamont*
MacCodrum *MacDonald*
MacColman *Buchanan*
MacComas *Gunn*
MacCombe *Mackintosh*
MacCombich *Stewart*
MacCombie *Mackintosh*
MacConacher *MacDougall*
MacConachie *MacGregor, Robertson*
MacCondy *MacFarlane*
MacConnach *MacKenzie*
MacConnechy *Campbell, Robertson*
MacConnell *MacDonald*
MacConnochie *Campbell, MacGregor, Robertson*
MacCook *MacDonald*
MacCorkill, MacCorkle *Gunn*
MacCorkindale *MacLeod*
MacCormack, MacCormick *Buchanan, MacLaine of Lochbuie*
MacCorquodale *MacLeod*
MacCorrie, MacCorry *Macquarrie*
MacCoull *MacDougall*
MacCowan *Colquhoun, MacDougall*
MacCracken *MacLean*

MacCrae, MacCrea *Macrae*
MacCrain *MacDonald*
MacCraw *Macrae*
MacCreath *Macrae*
MacCrie *MacKay, Macrae*
MacCrimmon *MacLeod of Harris*
MacCrowther *MacGregor*
MacCuag *MacDonald*
MacCuag *Farquharson, MacLeod of Harris*
MacCuish *MacDonald*
MacCulloch *MacDonald, MacDougall, Munro, Ross*
MacCunn *Macqueen*
MacCutchen, MacCutcheon *MacDonald*
MacDade, MacDaid *Davidson*
MacDaniel *MacDonald*
MacDavid *Davidson*
MacDermid *Campbell of Argyll*
MacDiarmid* *Campbell of Argyll*
MacDonachie *Robertson*
Macdonleavy *Buchanan*
MacDowall, MacDowell *MacDougall*
MacDuffie *Macfie*
MacEachan *MacDonald of Clanranald*
MacEachern, MacEacheran *MacDonald*
MacEaracher *Farquharson*
MacElheron *MacDonald*
MacErracher *Farquharson, MacFarlane*

MacFadyen*, MacFadzean *MacLaine of Lochbuie*
MacFall *Mackintosh*
MacFarquhar *Farquharson*
MacFatter *MacLaren*
MacFeat *MacLaren*
MacFergus *Ferguson*
MacGaw *MacFarlane*
MacGeachie *MacDonald of Clanranald*
MacGeachin *MacDonald*
MacGeoch *MacFarlane*
Macghee, Macghie *MacKay*
MacGibbon *Buchanan, Campbell, Graham*
MacGilbert *Buchanan*
MacGilchrist *MacLachlan, Ogilvie*
MacGill*
MacGilledow *Lamont*
MacGillegowie *Lamont*
MacGillivantic *MacDonell of Keppoch*
MacGillonie *Cameron*
MacGilp *MacDonell of Keppoch*
MacGilroy *Grant, MacGillivray*
MacGilvernock *Graham*
MacGilvray *MacGillivray*
Macglashan *Mackintosh, Stewart*
MacGorrie, MacGorry *MacDonald, Macquarrie*
MacGowan *see* Gow
Macgrath *Macrae*

MacGrory *MacLaren*
Macgrowther *MacGregor*
Macgruder *MacGregor*
Macgruer *Fraser*
Macgruther *MacGregor*
MacGuffie *Macfie*
MacGugan *MacDougall, MacNeill*
MacGuire *Macquarrie*
MacHaffie *Macfie*
MacHardie, MacHardy* *Farquharson, Mackintosh*
MacHarold *MacLeod of Harris*
MacHay *Mackintosh*
MacHendrie, MacHendry *Henderson, MacNaughton*
MacHenry *MacDonald*
MacHowell *MacDougall*
MacHugh *MacDonald*
MacHutchen, MacHutcheon *MacDonald*
MacIan* *Gunn, MacDonald*
Macildowie *Cameron*
Macilreach, Macilriach *MacDonald*
Macilrevie *MacDonald*
Macilroy *MacGillivray, Grant*
Macilvain *MacBean*
Macilvora *MacLaine of Lochbuie*
Macilvraie *MacGillivray*
MacIlvride *MacDonald*
MacIlwham *Lamont*
MacIlwraith *MacDonald*
Macimmey *Fraser*
MacInally *Buchanan*

232

MacIndeor *Buchanan,*
  Macnab, Menzies
Macindoe *Buchanan*
MacInroy* *Robertson*
Macinstalker *MacFarlane*
MacIsaac *Campbell,*
  MacDonald of Clanranald
MacJames *MacFarlane*
MacKail *Cameron*
MacKames *Gunn*
MacKeachan *MacDonald of*
  Clanranald
MacKeamish *Gunn*
MacKean *Gunn, MacDonald*
MacKechnie *MacDonald of*
  Clanranald
MacKee *MacKay*
Mackeggie *Mackintosh*
MacKeith *Keith, Macpherson*
MacKellaig *MacDonald*
MacKellar* *Campbell of*
  Argyll
MacKelloch *MacDonald*
MacKemmie *Fraser*
MacKendrick *see* Henderson
MacKeochan *MacDonald of*
  Clanranald
MacKerchar *Farquharson*
MacKerlich *MacKenzie*
MacKerrachar *Farquharson*
MacKerras *Ferguson*
MacKersey *Ferguson*
MacKessock *Campbell,*
  MacDonald of Clanranald
MacKichan *MacDonald of*
  Clanranald, MacDougall

Mackie *MacKay*
MacKiggan *MacDonald*
MacKillican *Mackintosh*
MacKillop *MacDonell of*
  Keppoch
MacKim, MacKimmie *Fraser*
Mackindlay *Farquharson*
Mackinlay* *Buchanan,*
  Farquharson, MacFarlane,
  Stewart
MacKinnell *MacDonald*
MacKinney *MacKinnon*
Mackinning *MacKinnon*
MacKinven *MacKinnon*
MacKirdy* *Stewart*
MacKissock *Campbell,*
  MacDonald of Clanranald
MacKnight *MacNaughton*
MacLagan *Robertson*
MacLaghlan *MacLachlan*
MacLamond *Lamont*
MacLardie, MacLardy
  MacDonald
MacLarty *MacDonald*
MacLaverty *MacDonald*
Maclay*, Macleay *Buchanan,*
  Stewart
MacLea *Stewart*
Maclehose *Campbell of*
  Argyll
Macleish *Macpherson*
MacLeister *Fletcher*
MacLellan *MacDonald*
MacLergain *MacLean*
MacLerie *Cameron,*
  Mackintosh, Macpherson

MacLewis *MacLeod, Stewart*
MacLintock* *Colquhoun*
MacLise *Macpherson*
MacLiver *MacGregor*
MacLucas *Lamont,*
   MacDougall
MacLugash *MacDougall*
MacLullich *MacDougall,*
   Munro, Ross
Maclure *MacLeod of Harris*
MacLymont *Lamont*
MacMartin *Cameron*
MacMaster *Buchanan,*
   MacInnes
MacMath *Matheson*
MacMaurice *Buchanan*
MacMenzies *Menzies*
MacMichael *Stewart*
MacMinn *Menzies*
MacMonnies *Menzies*
MacMordoch, MacMurdoch
   MacDonald, Macpherson
MacMorran *MacKinnon*
MacMunn *Stewart*
MacMurchie, MacMurchy
   Buchanan, MacDonald,
   MacKenzie
MacMurdo *MacDonald,*
   Macpherson
MacMurray *Murray*
MacMurrich *MacDonald of*
   Clanranald, Macpherson
MacMutrie *Stuart of Bute*
MacNair, MacNayer
   MacFarlane, MacNaughton
MacNee *MacGregor*

MacNeilage *MacNeill*
MacNeish *MacGregor*
MacNeilly, MacNelly
   MacNeill
MacNeur *MacFarlane*
MacNicol* *MacLeod*
MacNidder *MacFarlane*
MacNie *MacGregor*
MacNish *MacGregor*
MacNiven *Cumming,*
   Mackintosh, MacNaughton
MacNuyer *Buchanan,*
   MacFarlane, MacNaughton
MacOmie *Mackintosh*
MacOmish *Gunn*
MacOnie *Cameron*
MacOwan *Campbell*
MacPatrick *Lamont, MacLaren*
MacPeter *MacGregor*
MacPhail* *Cameron,*
   Mackintosh, MacKay
MacPhater *MacLaren*
MacPhedran *Campbell,*
   MacAulay
MacPhillips *MacDonell of*
   Keppoch
MacPhun *Campbell, Matheson*
Macquey, MacQuhae
   MacKay
Macquhirr *Macquarrie*
MacQuire *Macquarrie*
MacQuiston *MacDonald*
MacRaild *MacLeod of Harris*
MacRaith *MacDonald,*
   Macrae
MacRankin *MacLean*

234

MacRath *Macrae*
MacRitchie *Mackintosh*
MacRob, MacRobb *Gunn, Innes, MacFarlane, Robertson*
MacRobbie *Robertson*
MacRobert *Robertson*
MacRobie *Drummond, Robertson*
MacRorie, MacRory *MacDonald*
MacRuer *MacDonald*
MacRurie, MacRury *MacDonald*
MacShimmie *Fraser*
MacSimon *Fraser*
MacSorley *Cameron, Lamont, MacDonald*
MacSporran *MacDonald*
MacSuain *Macqueen*
MacSwan *MacDonald, Macqueen*
MacSween *Macqueen*
MacSymon *Fraser*
MacTaggart* *Ross*
MacTause *Campbell of Argyll*
MacTavish* *Campbell of Argyll*
MacTear *Macintyre, Ross*
MacThomas* *Campbell of Argyll, Mackintosh*
MacTier, MacTire *Ross*
MacUlric *Kennedy*
MacUre *Campbell of Argyll, MacIver*
MacVail *Cameron, MacKay, Mackintosh, Macpherson*
MacVarish *MacDonald of Clanranald*
MacVeagh *MacDonald, MacLean*
MacVean *MacBean*
MacVey *MacDonald, MacLean*
MacVicar *Campbell, MacNaughton*
MacVinish *MacKenzie*
MacVurie *MacDonald of Clanranald*
MacVurrich *MacDonald of Clanranald, Macpherson*
MacWalrick *Kennedy*
MacWalter *MacFarlane*
MacWattie *Buchanan*
MacWhannell *MacDonald*
MacWhirr *Macquarrie*
MacWhirter* *Buchanan*
MacWilliam* *Gunn, MacFarlane*
Maitland*
Malcolmson *MacCallum, MacLeod, Malcolm*
Malloch *MacGregor*
Mann *Gunn*
Manson *Gunn*
Marnoch *Innes*
Marr *Gordon*
Marshall *Keith*
Martin *Cameron, MacDonald*
Mason *Sinclair*
Masterson, Masterton *Buchanan*
Mathie *Matheson*

Maxwell*
May *MacDonald*
Means *Menzies*
Meikleham *Lamont*
Mein, Meine *Menzies*
Melvin *MacBeth*
Mengues *Menzies*
Mennie *Menzies*
Menteith *Graham, Stewart*
Meyners *Menzies*
Michie *Forbes*
Middleton* *Innes*
Miller *MacFarlane*
Milne *Gordon*
Minns, Minnus *Menzies*
Mitchell* *Innes*
Moir *Gordon*
Monach *MacFarlane*
Monteith *Graham, Stewart*
Monzie *Menzies*
Moray *Murray*
More *Leslie*
Morgan *MacKay*
Mowat* *Sutherland*
Muir*
Munn *Stewart*
Murchie *Buchanan,
    MacDonald, MacKenzie*
Murchison *Buchanan,
    MacDonald, MacKenzie*
Murdoch *MacDonald,
    Macpherson*
Murdoson *MacDonald,
    Macpherson*
Neal *MacNeill*
Neil, Neill *MacNeill*

Neilson *MacKay, MacNeill*
Neish *MacGregor*
Nelson *Gunn*
Nicol, Nicoll *MacNicol*
Nicolson *see* MacNicol
Nisbet*
Nish *MacGregor*
Niven *Cumming, Mackintosh,
    MacNaughton*
Noble *Mackintosh*
Norman *MacLeod of Harris*
Norrie *MacDonald*
Parlane *MacFarlane*
Paterson *MacLaren*
Patrick *Lamont*
Paul *Cameron, Mackintosh,
    MacKay*
Peter *MacGregor*
Philipson *MacDonell of
    Keppoch*
Piper *Murray of Atholl*
Pitullich *MacDonald*
Polson *MacKay*
Purcell *MacDonald*
Rae* *Macrae*
Raeburn*
Rankin* *MacLean*
Rattray* *Murray*
Reid *Murray, Robertson*
Reidford *Innes*
Reoch *Farquharson,
    MacDonald*
Revie *MacDonald*
Riach *Farquharson,
    MacDonald*
Risk *Buchanan*

236

Ritchie *Mackintosh*
Robb *MacFarlane, Robertson*
Robinson *Gunn*
Robison *Gunn*
Robson *Gunn*
Rollo*
Ronald, Ronaldson *MacDonell of Keppoch*
Rorison *MacDonald*
Roy *Robertson*
Ruskin *Buchanan*
Russell*
Ruthven*
Sanderson *MacDonell of Glengarry*
Sandison *Gunn*
Seaton, Seton*
Scobie *MacKay*
Shannon *MacDonald*
Sim, Sime *Fraser*
Simon *Fraser*
Simpson, Simson *Fraser*
Smail, Small *Murray*
Smith *MacKintosh*
Sorley *Cameron, Lamont, MacDonald*
Spalding *Murray*
Spence *MacDuff*
Spens *MacDuff*
Spittal *Buchanan*
Sporran *MacDonald*
Stalker *MacFarlane*
Stark *Robertson*
Sturrock*
Swan *Macqueen*

Swanson *Gunn*
Syme *Fraser*
Symon *Fraser*
Taggart *Ross*
Tarrell *Mackintosh*
Tawesson *Campbell of Argyll*
Tawse *Farquharson*
Thains *Innes*
Taylor* *Cameron*
Thomas *Campbell*
Thomason *Campbell, MacFarlane*
Thompson, Thomson* *Campbell*
Todd *Gordon*
Tolmie *MacLeod*
Tosh *Mackintosh*
Toshack *Mackintosh*
Toward, Towart *Lamont*
Train *MacDonald*
Turner *Lamont*
Tweedie *Fraser*
Tyre *Macintyre*
Ure *Campbell, MacIver*
Vass *Munro, Ross*
Wallis *Wallace*
Walters *Forbes*
Wass *Munro, Ross*
Watson *Buchanan*
Watt *Buchanan, Forbes*
Weaver *MacFarlane*
Weir* *Buchanan, MacFarlane, MacNaughton*
Wemyss* *MacDuff*
Whannell *MacDonald*
Wharrie *MacQuarrie*

White, Whyte *Lamont, MacGregor*
Wilkinson *MacDonald*
Will *Gunn*
Williamson *Gunn, MacKay*

Wilson* *Gunn*
Wotherspoon*
Wright *Macintyre*
Wylie *Gunn, MacFarlane*
Yuill, Yuille, Yule *Buchanan*

Sources of Further Information

Tartan Collections

The **Scottish Tartan Society**, Pitlochry, Perthshire contains probably the most extensive collection of tartans of all periods in existence, supplemented by a valuable library of books on the subject.

Other collections include:
The Cockburn Collection, The Mitchell Library, Glasgow
The Highland Society of London Collection, London
The West Highland Museum Collection, Fort William
The National Museum of Antiquities Collection, Edinburgh